# STUDY GUIDE

# Treasure Island
*Robert Louis Stevenson*

# WITH CONNECTIONS

**HOLT, RINEHART AND WINSTON**
*Harcourt Brace & Company*

**Austin** • New York • Orlando • Atlanta • San Francisco • Boston • Dallas • Toronto • London

## Staff Credits

**Associate Director:** Mescal Evler

**Manager of Editorial Operations:** Robert R. Hoyt

**Managing Editor:** Bill Wahlgren

**Executive Editor:** Emily Shenk

**Editor:** Cheryl Christian

**Editorial Staff:** *Assistant Managing Editor,* Mandy Beard; *Copyediting Supervisor,* Michael Neibergall; *Senior Copyeditor,* Mary Malone; *Copyeditors,* Joel Bourgeois, Jon Hall, Jeffrey T. Holt, Jane M. Kominek, Susan Sandoval; *Editorial Coordinators,* Marie H. Price, Jill Chertudi, Mark Holland, Marcus Johnson, Tracy DeMont; *Support Staff,* Pat Stover, Matthew Villalobos; *Word Processors,* Ruth Hooker, Margaret Sanchez, Kelly Keeley

**Permissions:** Carrie Jones, Catherine Paré

**Design:** *Art Director, Book & Media Design,* Joe Melomo

**Image Services:** *Art Buyer, Supervisor,* Elaine Tate

**Prepress Production:** Beth Prevelige, Sergio Durante

**Manufacturing Coordinator:** Michael Roche

*Development Coordinator:* Diane B. Engel

Copyright © by Holt, Rinehart and Winston

All rights reserved. No part of this publication may be reproduced or transmitted in any form or by any means, electronic or mechanical, including photocopy, recording, or any information storage and retrieval system, without permission in writing from the publisher.

Teachers using HRW LIBRARY may photocopy blackline masters in complete pages in sufficient quantities for classroom use only and not for resale.

**Cover illustration:** Brian Fox

HRW is a registered trademark licensed to Holt, Rinehart and Winston.

Printed in the United States of America

ISBN 0-03-054008-9

3456 085 02 01

# TABLE *of* CONTENTS

## FOR THE TEACHER

Using This Study Guide .................................................................................................................. 2

Tips for Classroom Management ................................................................................................. 3

Strategies for Inclusion ................................................................................................................. 4

Assessment Options ...................................................................................................................... 5

About the Writer ........................................................................................................................... 6

About the Novel ............................................................................................................................ 7

Key Elements: Plot / Theme / Characters / Setting / Point of View / Conflict ....................... 8–12

| Resources Overview ............... inside front cover | Answer Key ............ 57–69 |
|---|---|

## FOR THE STUDENT

Before You Read: Activities ........................................................................................................ 13

Chapters 1–6: Making Meanings / Choices ........................................................................... 14–15

Chapters 7–12: Making Meanings / Choices ......................................................................... 16–17

Chapters 13–21: Making Meanings / Choices ....................................................................... 18–19

Chapters 22–27: Making Meanings / Choices ....................................................................... 20–21

Chapters 28–34: Making Meanings / Choices ....................................................................... 22–23

**Novel Projects:** Cross-Curricular Connections / Multimedia and Internet Connections ...... 24–26

**Exploring the Connections:** Making Meanings

    The Mildenhall Treasure, by Roald Dahl ............................................................................. 27

    "We Found It! We Found It!" by Amy Wilentz .................................................................... 28

    Tiger Moran's Loot, from *The Mouse Rap,* by Walter Dean Myers ................................... 28

    Return to the *Titanic,* from *The Discovery of the Titanic,* by Robert D. Ballard ............. 29

**Novel Notes:** Issues 1–8 ....................................................................................................... 30–37

**Reading Skills and Strategies Worksheets:** Novel Organizer / Describing Characters / Responding to Quotations
    Tracking Plot Details / Identifying Problems and Solutions / Analyzing Events ............ 38–44

**Literary Elements Worksheets:** Plot / Characterization / Conflict ..................................... 45–47

Glossary ................................................................................................................................. 48–50

Vocabulary Worksheets ......................................................................................................... 51–52

Test ........................................................................................................................................ 53–56

Study Guide | **1**

# Using This Study Guide

**This Study Guide is intended to**
- *help students become active and engaged readers*
- *deepen students' enjoyment and understanding of literature*
- *provide you with multiple options for guiding students through the novel and the Connections and for evaluating students' progress*

*Most of the pages in this Study Guide are reproducible so that you can, if you choose, give students the opportunity to work independently.*

## Key Elements
- plot summary and analysis
- major themes
- character summaries
- notes on setting, point of view, and other literary elements

## Making Meanings
- First Thoughts
- Shaping Interpretations
- Connecting with the Text
- Extending the Text
- Challenging the Text

A **Reading Check** focuses on review and comprehension.

## The Worksheets
- **Reading Skills and Strategies Worksheets** focus on reading and critical-thinking strategies and skills.
- **Literary Elements Worksheets** guide students in considering and analyzing literary elements (discussed in **Key Elements**) important to understanding the novel.
- **Vocabulary Worksheets** provide practice with Vocabulary Words. Activities target synonyms, affixes, roots, context clues, and other vocabulary elements.

## For the Teacher

**About the Writer** Biographical highlights supplement the author biography that appears in the HRW Library edition of this novel. Sidebars list works by and about the writer as resources for teaching and for students' research.

**About the Novel** A critical history summarizes responses to the novel, including excerpts from reviews. Sidebars suggest audiovisual and multimedia resources.

**Key Elements** Significant literary elements of the novel are introduced. These elements recur in the questions, activities, worksheets, and assessment tools.

## For the Student: reproducible masters

**Before You Read: Activities** *(preparation for beginning the novel)*
Motivating activities lead students to explore ideas and topics they will encounter in the novel.

**Making Meanings** *(for each section of the novel)* Questions move students from immediate personal response to high-level critical thinking.

**Choices: Building Your Portfolio** *(for each section of the novel)* The activities suggested here involve students in exploring different aspects of the novel on their own or collaboratively. The results may be included in a portfolio, developed further, or used as springboards for larger projects.

**Novel Projects** *(culminating activities)* Cross-Curricular, Multimedia, and Internet projects relate to the novel as a whole. Project ideas can be adapted for individual, pair, or group presentations.

**Exploring the Connections** *(a set of Making Meanings questions for each of the Connections readings)* Questions encourage students to relate the readings to the themes and topics of the novel.

**Novel Notes** *(multiple issues)* These one-page news sheets provide high-interest background information relating to historical, cultural, literary, and other elements of the novel. They are intended for distribution *after* students have begun the novel section the issue supplements.

**Reading Skills and Strategies Worksheets** *(one for each section of the novel, plus a Novel Organizer)*

**Literary Elements Worksheets** *(end of novel)*

**Vocabulary Worksheets** *(during or after reading)*

**Glossary, with Vocabulary Words** *(to use throughout the novel)* This list of words from the novel serves as a mini-dictionary that students may refer to as they read. **Highlighted Vocabulary Words** support vocabulary acquisition.

**Test** *(end of novel)* A mix of objective and short-answer questions covering the whole novel provides a traditional form of assessment. Essay questions consist of five optional writing prompts.

# Tips for Classroom Management

## Preparing Students for Reading
Set aside a time each week for talking about books. On the right are some ideas for introducing a novel and motivating students to pick it up and begin reading.

## Reading and Responding
**Book groups** Although most students will read independently, discussions with classmates can enrich their reading enormously. This Study Guide suggests appropriate points to stop and talk about the story so far. At these stopping points, the **Making Meanings** questions can be used as discussion starters. Ask groups to keep a simple log of their discussions.

**Full-class discussions** Engage students by beginning the discussion with a question that encourages a personal response (see **First Thoughts** in **Making Meanings**). As students respond to the questions involving interpretation, invite them to support their inferences and conclusions with evidence from the text. Encourage a noncritical environment. Show your own enthusiasm for the novel—it's infectious!

**Reader's logs** Logs, journals, and notebooks offer an open and nonthreatening yet systematic mode for students to respond in writing to the novel. Making entries as they read can help students learn more about themselves as readers, monitor their own progress, and write more easily and fluently. Keeping logs can also enhance participation in small-group and class discussions of the novel. Consider dialogue journals in which two readers—a student and you, a classmate, or a family member—exchange thoughts about their reading. **Reader's Log** suggestions appear in each issue of **Novel Notes**.

**Cooperative learning** Small groups may meet both to discuss the novel and to plan and work on projects related to the novel (see ideas in **Choices** and in **Novel Projects**). Encourage full participation by making sure that each group member has a defined role and that the roles rotate so that the same student is not always the leader or the recorder, for example.

**Projects** While students' projects can extend into other content areas, they should always contribute to enriching and extending students' understanding of the novel itself. If students know when they begin the novel that presenting a project will be a part of their evaluation, they can begin early to brainstorm, discuss, and try out ideas. Project ideas can come from **Novel Notes**, from the **Choices** activities, from the **Novel Projects** ideas, and, of course, from the students themselves. Projects can be developed and presented by individuals, pairs, or groups.

## Reflecting
When students finish the novel, they should not be left with a test as the culminating experience. Project presentations can be a kind of celebration, as can a concluding discussion. On the right are some ideas for a reflective discussion. They can be used in a whole-class environment, or small groups can choose certain questions to answer and share their conclusions (or their disagreements) with the class.

### Ideas for Introducing the Novel
- Give a brief book talk to arouse students' curiosity and interest (see **About the Novel** for ideas).
- Play or show a segment of an audio, film, or video version of the book or an interview with the writer.
- Present high-interest biographical information about the writer (see **About the Writer** in this Study Guide and the biographical sketch at the end of the HRW Library edition of this novel).
- Read aloud a passage from the novel that arouses your own interest, and elicit predictions, inferences, and speculations from students.
- Lead a focused class discussion or suggest activities that (1) draw on students' prior knowledge or (2) lead them to generate their own ideas about a significant topic or theme they will encounter in the novel (see **Before You Read**).

### Reader's Log Starters
- When I began reading this book, I thought...
- My favorite part, so far, is...
- I predict that...
- I like the way the writer...
- I'd like to ask the writer...
- If I had written this book, I would have...
- This [character, incident, idea] reminds me of...
- This book made me think about...
- This book made me realize...

### Questions for Reflection
- What was your favorite part of the book (and why)?
- If you could be one of the characters, who would it be (and why)?
- Would you or wouldn't you recommend this book to a friend (and why)?
- What is the most important thing about this book?
- Would you change the ending? If not, what makes it work? If yes, what changes would you make?
- If you could have a conversation with the writer, what would you say or ask?

# Strategies for Inclusion

*Each set of activities has been developed to meet special student interests, abilities, and learning styles. Because the questions and activities in this Study Guide are directed to the students, there are no labels to indicate the types of learners they target. However, in each* Before You Read, Choices, *and* Novel Projects *page, you will find activities to meet the needs of*

- *less proficient readers*
- *students acquiring English*
- *advanced students*

*The activities and projects have been prepared to accommodate these different learning styles:*

- *auditory/musical*
- *interpersonal*
- *intrapersonal*
- *kinesthetic*
- *logical/mathematical*
- *verbal/linguistic*
- *visual/spatial*

## Using the Study Guide Questions and Activities

Encourage students to adapt the suggestions given in the Study Guide to fit their own learning styles and interests. It is important to remember that students are full of surprises, and a question or activity that is challenging to an advanced student can also be handled successfully by students who are less proficient readers. The high interest level, flexibility, and variety of these questions and activities make them appropriate for a range of students.

Students should be encouraged to vary the types of activities they choose so that the same student is not regularly selecting writing or researching activities over those involving speaking, art, and performing, and vice versa. Individual and group work should also alternate, so that students have the opportunity to work on their own and as part of collaborative learning groups.

## Working in Pairs and Groups

When students with varying abilities, cultural backgrounds, and learning styles work together, they can arrive at a deeper understanding of both the novel and one another.

Reading pairs can stop and check each other's responses to the novel at frequent intervals.

Students from different cultural groups can interview one another about how certain situations, character interactions, character motivations, and so on would be viewed in their home cultures.

## Visualizing and Performing

Students who have difficulty with writing or with presenting their ideas orally can demonstrate their understanding of the novel in a variety of ways:

- making cluster diagrams or sketching their ideas

- creating tableaux showing where characters are in relation to one another during a scene, their poses or stances, and their facial expressions

- creating thought balloons with drawings or phrases that show what a character is thinking at a given moment

- drawing their own thoughts in thought balloons above a sketched self-portrait

- listing or drawing images that come to mind as they read or hear a certain section or passage of the novel

- making a comic-book version of the novel (with or without words)

- coming to class as a character in the novel

# Assessment Options

Perhaps the most important goal of assessment is to inform instruction. As you monitor the degree to which your students understand and engage with the novel, you will naturally modify your instructional plan. The frequency and balance of class and small-group discussion, the time allowed for activities, and the extent to which direct teaching of reading skills and strategies, literary elements, or vocabulary is appropriate can all be planned on the basis of your ongoing assessment of your students' needs.

Several forms of assessment are particularly appropriate for work with the novel:

**Observing and note taking** Anecdotal records that reflect both the degree and the quality of students' participation in class and small-group discussions and activities will help you target areas in which coaching or intervention is appropriate. Because communication skills are such an integral part of working with the novel in a classroom setting, it is appropriate to evaluate the process of making meaning in this social context.

**Involving yourself with dialogue journals and letters** You may want to exchange notes with students instead of, or in addition to, encouraging them to keep reader's logs. A powerful advantage of this strategy is that at the same time you have the opportunity to evaluate students' responses, you can make a significant difference in the quality of the response. When students are aware that their comments are valued (and addressed to a real audience, an audience that writes back), they often wake up to the significance of what they are reading and begin to make stronger connections between the text and their own lives.

**Agreeing on criteria for evaluation** If evaluation is to be fair, it must be predictable. As students propose and plan an activity or project, collaborate with them to set up the criteria by which their work will be evaluated, and be consistent in applying only those criteria.

**Encouraging self-evaluation and goal setting** When students are partners with you in creating criteria for evaluation, they can apply those criteria to their own work. You might ask them to rate themselves on a simple scale of 1, 2, or 3 for each of the criteria and to arrive at an overall score. Students can then set goals based on self-evaluation.

**Peer evaluation** Students can participate in evaluating one another's demonstrations and presentations, basing their evaluations upon a previously established set of standards. Modeling a peer-evaluation session will help students learn this method, and a chart or checklist can guide peer discussion. Encourage students to be objective, sensitive, courteous, and constructive in their comments.

**Keeping portfolios** If you are in an environment where portfolios contain only carefully chosen samples of students' writing, you may want to introduce a second, "working," portfolio and negotiate grades with students after examining all or selected items from these portfolios.

### Opportunities for Assessment

The suggestions in this Study Guide provide multiple opportunities for assessment across a range of skills:

- demonstrating reading comprehension
- keeping reader's logs
- listening and speaking
- working in groups—both discussion and activity-oriented
- planning, developing, and presenting a final project
- acquiring vocabulary
- taking tests

### Questions for Self-evaluation and Goal Setting

- What are the three most important things I learned in my work with this novel?
- How will I follow up with these so that I remember them?
- What was the most difficult part of working with this novel?
- How did I deal with the difficulty, and what would I do differently?
- What two goals will I work toward in my [reading/writing/group work, etc.]?
- What steps will I take to achieve those goals?

### Items for a "Working" Portfolio

- reading records
- drafts of written work and project plans
- audio- and videotapes of presentations
- notes on discussions
- reminders of cooperative projects, such as planning and discussion notes
- artwork
- objects and mementos connected with themes and topics in the novel
- other evidence of engagement with the book

*For help with establishing and maintaining portfolio assessment, examine the* **Portfolio Management System** *in* **Elements of Literature.**

# About the Writer — Robert Louis Stevenson

## More on Stevenson

Calder, Jenni. **Robert Louis Stevenson: A Life Study.** New York: Oxford University Press, 1980. A critical biography with interesting background on the writing of *Treasure Island*.

Eigner, Edwin M. **Robert Louis Stevenson and Romantic Tradition.** Princeton, NJ: Princeton University Press, 1966. This useful study of Stevenson and his relationship to the romantic tradition includes a chapter on *Treasure Island*.

Gherman, Beverly. **Robert Louis Stevenson: Teller of Tales.** New York: Atheneum, 1996. This young adult biography stresses Stevenson's travels and his willingness to buck tradition in his career choices.

McLynn, Frank. **Robert Louis Stevenson: A Biography.** New York: Random House, 1994. A recent study.

Saposnik, Irving S. **Robert Louis Stevenson.** New York: Twayne, 1974. Part of Twayne's English Authors Series.

## Also by Stevenson

**The Body Snatcher** (1885). As the title suggests, this is a thrilling tale of grave robbery.

**An Inland Voyage** (1878), **Travels with a Donkey in the Cévennes** (1879), and **The Silverado Squatters** (1883). These three travel books characterize the charm and style of Stevenson's nonfiction work.

**Kidnapped** (1886). After David Balfour, an orphan, is kidnapped by his uncle, he escapes and becomes involved in the Scottish Highlanders' struggle for independence.

**The Strange Case of Dr. Jekyll and Mr. Hyde** (1886). While studying dual personalities, the kindly Dr. Jekyll invents a potion that changes him into the evil and violent Mr. Hyde.

---

*A biography of Robert Louis Stevenson appears in* Treasure Island, *HRW Library Edition. You may wish to share this additional biographical information with your students.*

Many aspects of Robert Louis Stevenson's life would qualify him as a "wanderer." His career choice provides an example. Stevenson's father and grandfather were famous lighthouse engineers. Stevenson tried to follow in their footsteps by entering Edinburgh University at the age of seventeen to study civil engineering. He lost interest in engineering, though, and switched to law. Although he did become an attorney, he never practiced law. Instead—much to his father's displeasure—he turned to writing.

Rather than settling down in one place, Stevenson "wandered," journeying from Europe to the United States to Australia and the South Seas. Sometimes he traveled to find relief from the tuberculosis that had plagued him from childhood. Sometimes he traveled in spite of the strain that it put on his health. Once he traveled for love—again, against his family's wishes—going to California to see Fanny Osbourne, the woman he would marry.

Despite some of his personal "wanderings," Stevenson persisted in his greatest goal—to be a novelist. He had had some success with essays, short stories, and travel books. He had attempted novels at least a dozen times. It was not until he found the inspiration for *Treasure Island,* however, that Stevenson was able to meet his goal—not just once, but with many novels afterward.

# About the Novel

*Treasure Island*

Stevenson intended *Treasure Island* as an adventure story for boys. He first got it published as a series in *Young Folks* magazine between October 1, 1881, and January 28, 1882, under the pseudonym Captain George North.

Surprisingly, the story was not very popular in its magazine form, even among the young readers for whom it was written. Stevenson conceded that it "appeared duly in the story paper, where it figured in the ignoble midst, without woodcuts, and attracted not the least attention." In 1883, however, it was reprinted in book form under Stevenson's name. Over the years, *Treasure Island* has won lasting popularity among readers and critics alike.

## CRITICAL COMMENT

> *Treasure Island* has been widely admired as an adventure story for young readers, but many critics regard it as something more. No less a critic than Henry James called it a "classic." *Treasure Island* has been praised in particular for its wonderful characterization, fast-moving and well-crafted plot, evocative descriptive passages, and realistic dialogue.
>
> Despite the praise, some critics have taken issue with its violence and the roughness of its characters. An early reviewer for the *Dial* asserted that "there is no appreciable good accomplished by the book. It is a picture of the roughest phases of sea-life. . . . It will be relished by adventure-loving boys, but whether it will be wholesome reading for them is more than doubtful." Other critics acknowledge the content but interpret it differently. A reviewer for *The Literary World* in 1884 commented that "though there is rough talk in it, and rum, and murder, and assassination in cold blood, and suggestions of horrors untold, yet the materials are so subordinated to the treatment, and the art of the writer is so perfect, that the effect does not become shocking. . . . piracy is a fact, and this picture of it is graphic and obviously true."

## For Viewing

***Treasure Island.*** MGM, 1934. Classic film treatment of the novel, starring Wallace Beery, Jackie Cooper, and Lionel Barrymore.

***Treasure Island.*** Walt Disney Productions, 1950. Highly praised Disney adaptation of the novel.

***Treasure Island.*** Made for TV, 1990. All-star cast featuring Charlton Heston, Christian Bale, Oliver Reed, and Christopher Lee.

## For Listening

***Treasure Island.*** Random House Audio, 1993. Part of Everyman's Library Children's Classics series.

***Treasure Island.*** Dove Audio, 1996. Narrated by Michael York.

# Key Elements

*Treasure Island*

## Make a Connection

Invite student volunteers to discuss times when a person was involved in something he or she suspected was not right. How did that person handle the situation? Ask students to list the series of events that led to avoiding potential trouble.

A **Literary Elements Worksheet** that focuses on plot appears on page 45 of this Study Guide.

## Plot

***Chapters 1–6*** An elderly pirate, Billy Bones, comes to stay at the inn owned by Jim Hawkins's parents. When Bones's former shipmates discover him, he has a stroke and dies. Jim and his mother search the captain's sea-chest to retrieve payment for his debt to the inn. Before they finish, however, more seamen appear. Grabbing a packet, Jim flees with his mother. He gives the packet to Dr. Livesey, who opens it in the presence of Jim and the local squire. When they find a treasure map, they decide to search for the treasure.

***Chapters 7–12*** Preparations for the voyage are made, and Jim sails with Squire Trelawney and Dr. Livesey. Although Jim suspects the integrity of the cook, Long John Silver, Silver is amiable and convincing as an honest seaman. During the voyage to Treasure Island, Jim discovers that the crew is made up mainly of pirates, and Silver is their leader. They plan to take the treasure and the ship, and to kill Jim and the others. When Jim shares the information with Trelawney, Dr. Livesey, and Captain Smollett, they make plans to defend themselves.

***Chapters 13–21*** After the ship reaches Treasure Island, Captain Smollett allows the crew to go ashore. Jim sneaks along and witnesses the death of a loyal sailor. He runs away and meets Ben Gunn, a pirate who was marooned on the island three years before. Dr. Livesey, who remained on the *Hispaniola,* now picks up the narrative. He recounts how he, Trelawney, Smollett, and their comrades go ashore and take refuge in a stockade. The pirates attack and are fought off. Jim picks up the narrative and then rejoins his friends. The following morning, Silver comes to the stockade to bargain for the treasure map. He is refused, and the pirates attack. Several men are killed on both sides, and the captain is severely wounded.

***Chapters 22–27*** After the battle, Dr. Livesey goes to find Ben Gunn; Jim sneaks away to find Gunn's boat. He paddles to the *Hispaniola* and cuts it loose. He boards the ship and is attacked by the pirate Hands on board the ship. In the struggle, Jim is wounded but shoots Hands. Jim then returns to the stockade but finds it occupied by the pirates, who capture him.

**8** | *Treasure Island*

# Key Elements (continued)

*Treasure Island*

***Chapters 28–34*** Jim learns that his friends have given the blockhouse and map to the pirates. The pirates then go in search of the treasure but discover an empty hole. Furious, they attack Silver, but Dr. Livesey and the others chase them off. With Silver, they return to Ben Gunn's cave. Gunn had found the treasure and taken it there. They load the gold onto the *Hispaniola* and set sail, marooning the three remaining pirates. Silver escapes on the way home. Back in England, they divide up the treasure.

***Plot Structure*** Stevenson's **plot**—the series of events that make up his story—builds upon the discovery of a treasure map and the effort to recover the treasure. Complications arise when the crew is found to be unreliable. Events reach a **climax** when the crew of pirates discover that the treasure has been removed. Blaming their misfortune on Silver and Jim, the pirates begin to charge the two. The plot rushes to its **resolution** when Dr. Livesey and friends overcome the pirates and he reveals that the treasure is safe in a cave.

For information on **conflict,** see p.12.

## Theme

Students will see the following **themes,** or main ideas, developed in detail in *Treasure Island*.

***The Struggle Between Two Opposing Forces*** *Treasure Island* is a stage upon which the struggle between two opposing groups is played out in its most extreme and most subtle forms. Jim, along with his friends, and Long John Silver with his band of pirates are at opposite ends of this conflict. Both groups seek the treasure, but neither group is entirely good or totally evil. Trelawney may believe he intends good, but he is greedy for what once was taken from someone else. While Silver can be violent, deceptive, and ruthless, his amiability and vitality make him appealing. When he becomes the target of his own crew's evil intentions, it is difficult to avoid rooting for him.

### Make a Connection

Have students discuss a time when they have had to struggle for something they wanted. What obstacles did they have to overcome? What did they learn from their experiences?

**Connecting with *Elements of Literature***

You can use *Treasure Island* to extend students' examination of the themes and topics presented in *Elements of Literature*.

- *Introductory Course:* "Moments of Truth," Collection One
- *First Course:* "Do the Right Thing," Collection Three
- *Second Course:* "We All Need Somebody to Lean On," Collection One

Study Guide | **9**

# Key Elements *(continued)*

*Treasure Island*

***From Innocence to Maturity*** In many respects, this is a novel of initiation. The narrator, Jim Hawkins, is first seen as an innocent youth helping his parents take care of the family inn. Soon after Billy Bones arrives, however, Jim's innocence begins to fall away. He experiences the deaths of his father and of Bones and then the threat to his own and his mother's lives. He's whisked, unknowing, into a terrifying world of deception and greed. By the novel's end, Jim has changed. He has learned to see through the pirates' deception. In a larger sense, he is no longer innocent of the darkness in humanity.

***The Power of Greed*** Greed is both a principal theme and a strong motivating factor, continually advancing the plot. Both the treasure seekers and the mutineers are urged on by their greed. Not even the marooned Ben Gunn is immune to the powerful effects of greed.

## Characters

Like a police sketch artist, Stevenson produces vivid **character** portraits with just a few deft strokes of the pen. Stevenson creates a dominant impression by identifying and describing the outstanding, unique highlights of the character. He also tends to catch his characters on the run, rather than breaking up the plot progression for an extended description. An example of these **characterization** techniques occurs in the first paragraphs of Chapter 1, when Jim Hawkins describes Billy Bones upon the pirate's arrival at the Admiral Benbow. In Chapter 8, Long John Silver is introduced as "very tall and strong, with a face as big as a ham . . . whistling as he moved about among the tables." In this manner, the reader can visualize the character without losing track of the narrative.

Students will meet the following major **characters** in *Treasure Island*.

**Jim Hawkins** is a youth who helps his parents run the Admiral Benbow, an inn in England, and later sails in search of buried treasure. Jim narrates most of the story.

**Billy Bones,** an elderly pirate who comes to live at the Admiral Benbow, was previously Captain Flint's first mate.

**Long John Silver,** the one-legged pirate hired as cook for the voyage, was formerly quartermaster of Captain Flint's pirate crew. He is now the leader of the mutineers.

**Dr. Livesey** takes care of Jim's sick father and later provides leadership during the voyage.

---

**Make a Connection**

Ask students whether they think that people can be totally evil or totally good. Encourage them to give reasons and perhaps examples to support their answers.

A **Literary Elements Worksheet** that focuses on characterization appears on page 46 of this Study Guide.

# Key Elements (continued)

*Treasure Island*

**John Trelawney,** a local squire, purchases the schooner and organizes the voyage.

**Captain Smollett** is hired by Trelawney as captain of the *Hispaniola*.

**Ben Gunn** is a pirate who was marooned on Treasure Island.

**Captain Flint** was a famous pirate who buried his loot on Treasure Island. Captain Flint is also the name of Long John Silver's parrot.

## Setting

Although *Treasure Island* is romantic fiction, it must contain enough realism to enable readers to step into the action quickly and enjoy the adventure. A realistic **setting** contributes to the story's believability. Stevenson has Jim writing the story in the eighteenth century and sets the action in a time when pirates actually roamed the seas and secured treasure. The story begins at the Admiral Benbow, an inn on the English coast near the port of Bristol. The narrative proceeds aboard the schooner *Hispaniola* and then on the fictitious Treasure Island.

## Point of View

*Treasure Island* has been criticized for its inconsistent **point of view**. The first fifteen chapters are told in the **first person** by Jim Hawkins. Then Dr. Livesey takes over for three chapters before Jim returns. Two possible explanations for the switch include the following: (1) By giving the narrative to Dr. Livesey, Stevenson can continue using first-person point of view while Jim is absent from the ship. (2) The first fifteen chapters began to appear serially in a magazine before the later chapters were written, forcing Stevenson to live with early decisions affecting point of view.

**Make a Connection**

Call on volunteers to name any books, films, television programs, or even song lyrics that make use of a **first-person** narrator. Discuss the benefits and limitations of storytelling from this **point of view.**

Study Guide | 11

# Key Elements (continued)

*Treasure Island*

### Make a Connection

Have students name a film or television program with which they all are familiar. Discuss its **external conflicts** and **internal conflicts**. Encourage students to look for external and internal conflicts while reading *Treasure Island*.

A *Literary Elements Worksheet* that focuses on conflict appears on page 47 of this Study Guide.

## Conflict

Stevenson develops multiple layers of **conflict** within the plot of *Treasure Island*. The principal conflicts in the novel are **external**—between characters or forces—and include those between

- Billy Bones and his former shipmates from the *Walrus*
- Jim and his mother and the pirates who hunt for them following Bones's death
- the loyal crew and the mutineers
- Long John Silver and the mutineers
- Jim and Israel Hands in their deadly battle aboard the *Hispaniola*

Among these external conflicts, Stevenson interlaces **internal** conflicts. For example, as Jim lies under the bridge with his mother, he is caught between his fear of the pirates and his curiosity over what is happening. Silver faces internal conflict as he considers whether to save his neck by protecting Jim or to continue his attempt to retain leadership of the pirates and recover the treasure.

# Before You Read

*Treasure Island*

## Activities

**BUILDING ON PRIOR KNOWLEDGE**

### Pirates!

Get together with a partner and discuss what you know about pirates. Draw a cluster diagram of words and phrases about the topic. Add to the diagram as you read.

**MAKING PERSONAL CONNECTIONS**

### I've Got a Secret

With a small group of students, imagine that you have found a treasure map that will lead you to a hoard of pirate gold buried on a remote island. No one else knows that you have this map. Consider what you would do with this discovery. Would you show the map to trusted friends? How would you go about finding and recovering the treasure? Then, freewrite individually for a few minutes about one or more courses of action. Share your responses with the group.

**QUICKWRITE**

### Piracy Then and Now

*Treasure Island* takes place during the eighteenth century when pirates roamed the seas, preying on maritime shipping and sometimes ravaging coastal towns. Could similar events happen today? Quickwrite about your thoughts.

**COOPERATIVE LEARNING**

### Help Wanted

With three other students, imagine that you want to take a sea voyage. Assume, too, that there is a problem: you know nothing about sailing! Therefore, you must hire a crew to sail the ship. Figure out how you would go about selecting members of your crew. Answer the following questions:

- What shipboard jobs would the crew need to fill?
- What skills would the crew need?
- How could the crew's trustworthiness be evaluated?

One group member should lead the discussion, another should take notes, another should keep watch on time, and another should present the group's solution to the class.

### Novel Notes

Use **Novel Notes, Issue 1**

- to find out more about some of the topics in *Treasure Island*
- to get ideas for writing activities and other projects that will take you deeper into the book

Study Guide  **13**

# Chapters 1–6

## *Treasure Island*

## Making Meanings

### First Thoughts

1. What is your opinion of Billy Bones? Is he someone you would like to know? Why or why not?

### Shaping Interpretations

2. *Treasure Island* is told from the **first-person point of view.** Most of the story is told by Jim, who uses the first-person pronoun *I*. In your opinion, what effect does this point of view have on these chapters? How would they be different if told from the **third-person point of view**?

3. Describe Dr. Livesey's personality.

4. **Mood** is the feeling a piece of writing creates. How is the **mood** in the squire's hall different from the earlier mood at the Admiral Benbow?

5. What do these chapters suggest about greed? About the struggle between two opposing forces? List some story details that illustrate these **themes,** or main ideas.

### Connecting with the Text

6. Think about how Jim reacts to Black Dog, Pew, and the other pirates. If you had been in his place, how would you have reacted?

### Extending the Text

7. Following a treasure map is a perfect example of a "get-rich-quick" idea—that is, a plan to get a lifetime of wealth from just a little bit of work. What "get-rich-quick" ideas attract people today?

### Challenging the Text

8. Stevenson creates a convincing, powerful portrait of Billy Bones. Why do you think Stevenson worked so hard on this character, only to kill him off in Chapter 3?

---

**READING CHECK**

a. Why does Billy Bones prefer an inn without many guests?
b. What happens when Black Dog appears at the inn?
c. Why does Jim take the blind beggar to see Billy Bones?
d. When they realize that Billy Bones is dead, what do Jim and his mother do first? Why?
e. What does Jim do with the packet of papers? Why?

# Chapters 1–6 (continued)

## Treasure Island

# Choices: Building Your Portfolio

**LIST**

## What's Next?
Stevenson sets the stage for *Treasure Island* in the opening chapters. Can you figure out what will happen next? Discuss your predictions with a partner. Together, make a list, being as specific as you can. Then, share your list with other students. Are any predictions on both lists, or are the lists completely different?

**DICTIONARY**

## Bully for Billy
Billy Bones is a colorful character. His language is colorful, too—full of references to ships and sailing, and spiced with a seaman's language. Create a glossary of "Billy Words" that are new to you. Include a drawing, if you wish.

**SOUNDTRACK**

## *Treasure Island* Soundtrack
Imagine that your school theater group is planning to present *Treasure Island* as a play. You have been named music director. What music would you use for the events in these first few chapters? Parts of movie soundtracks? Classical music? Popular songs? Choose or write one or two pieces. Then, play the music for the class and explain your choices.

**CREATIVE WRITING**

## The Story of the Map
What's the story behind Bones's treasure map? How did he get the map? Do the other pirates have any right to claim it? Brainstorm about the history of the map; then, write a short-short story about it. Consider adding your story to your writing portfolio.

## *Consider This . . .*
*Pew's anger rose so high at these objections; till at last, his passion completely taking the upper hand, he struck at them right and left in his blindness, and his stick sounded heavily on more than one.*

Like Billy Bones, Pew cannot control his emotions. Can you imagine an anger this strong? How well do you think someone this angry would be able to act in a crisis?

### *Writing Follow-up: Problem Solving*

How should Jim deal with the two angry sailors he meets? Describe solutions to dealing with Billy Bones and Pew.

### Novel Notes

Use **Novel Notes, Issue 2**

- to find out more about some of the topics and themes in Chapters 1–6
- to get ideas for writing activities and other projects related to *Treasure Island*

Study Guide

# Chapters 7–12

## *Treasure Island*

# Making Meanings

### First Thoughts
1. How do you feel about Long John Silver being trusted to be ship's cook?

### Shaping Interpretations
2. Think about Jim's return visit to the Admiral Benbow to visit his mother. Do you see any evidence that Jim is growing up? Explain.

3. What sort of person is Captain Smollett? Compare his **character** to that of Dr. Livesey.

**READING CHECK**

a. Describe what Trelawney accomplished in Bristol.
b. What two facts make Jim suspicious of Long John Silver? What makes him decide that Silver is not dangerous?
c. What happens to Jim when he visits the apple barrel?
d. What reasons does Silver give to persuade the other pirates not to take over the ship immediately?

4. Silver wants to delay killing the captain, but he knows that he must do it soon in order to satisfy the other pirates. What do these details suggest about Silver's personality?

5. In Chapter 12, Silver tells Jim that he will have a pleasant time exploring the island. In your opinion, why does Silver talk to Jim in this way?

### Connecting with the Text
6. Jim arrives in Bristol ready for adventure. When he learns of Silver's planned mutiny, however, his attitude changes. Have you ever looked forward to something, only to have your hopes dashed? What words might describe those feelings?

### Extending the Text
7. As Chapter 12 closes, the members of the "council of war" try to figure out which of the crew will support them and which will not. How do you think most people decide who are their friends and who are their enemies?

### Challenging the Text
8. Smollett, Trelawney, and Livesey are intelligent people. Does it seem likely that they would be foolish enough to sail with a crew about whom they knew so little?

# Chapters 7–12 (continued)

## *Treasure Island*

# Choices: Building Your Portfolio

**PERFORMANCE OF SCENE**

## Casting Call
Team up with several classmates to explore the rich **dialogue** and **descriptions** in *Treasure Island*. Choose a scene and read it carefully. Study the actions and personalities of the **characters**. Then, divide up roles and perform the scene. Include a **narrator,** if you wish. Try to speak and act like the characters. Afterward, talk with the class about how it felt to "be" these characters and speak their language.

**SMALL GROUP DISCUSSION**

## What's Your Question
Working with three classmates, take turns reading aloud a short **scene** from this section of *Treasure Island*. Then, discuss the scene with your partners. Tell in your own words what happens. Identify the **characters** and explain their actions. Then, each of you should write a question about the events that came right before this scene. Exchange questions and take turns answering them.

**CRITICAL WRITING**

## Mistakes in Logic
In his letter to Dr. Livesey in Chapter 7, Squire Trelawney carefully describes how he acquired a ship and found a crew. Write a few paragraphs in which you review his letter and identify each of the squire's mistakes. Compare your results with those of other students.

**CREATIVE WRITING**

## Songs of the Sea
Songs were an important form of entertainment for sailors. Imagine yourself on a sailing ship. Your shipmates have challenged each other to a songwriting contest. Write the lyrics for a song. Use the tune of a song that you already know, or an original tune. Share your songs with your classmates. Who would be the winners, and why?

## Consider This . . .
*I began to feel pretty desperate at this, for I felt altogether helpless; and yet, by an odd train of circumstances, it was indeed through me that safety came.*

Jim has just told his comrades the crew's horrible secret. In return, they have given him a heavy responsibility. How does Jim feel now? How would you feel in his place?

### Writing Follow-up: Reflecting

Think of a time when you or someone you know felt uneasy at taking on a difficult task. How was that situation handled? In what ways did it resemble and differ from Jim's situation?

### Novel Notes

Use **Novel Notes, Issue 3**

- to find out more about some of the topics and themes in Chapters 7–12
- to get ideas for writing activities and other projects related to *Treasure Island*

Study Guide | **17**

# Chapters 13–21

## *Treasure Island*

## Making Meanings

### *First Thoughts*

1. In your opinion, how well can the pirates organize and follow through with a plan?

### *Shaping Interpretations*

2. Do you think Captain Smollett made a wise decision in allowing the crew to go ashore? Why or why not?

3. Compare Jim Hawkins and Dr. Livesey as **narrators,** or storytellers.

4. Think about the end of the first day's fighting. On that day, how do Captain Smollett and Tom Redruth demonstrate their dedication to duty?

5. How does raising the flag affect the men in the stockade? What does the flag seem to **symbolize,** or represent?

> **READING CHECK**
>
> a. When he first goes ashore, what does Jim witness happening between Silver and the sailor Tom?
> b. What does Dr. Livesey decide to do after inspecting the stockade, and why?
> c. What happens to the jolly-boat used by the doctor and others on their final trip to shore? Why does it happen?
> d. Silver visits the stockade under the flag of truce. What does he want? What does he offer in exchange?
> e. When the pirates attack, why is Captain Smollett confident that he and his companions can defend themselves?

6. Has the **character** of Jim changed in the course of the novel so far? Explain.

### *Connecting with the Text*

7. Suppose that you could step into the novel at this point and ask any of the characters a question. With whom would you speak? What would you want to know?

### *Extending the Text*

8. Mutiny is such a severe crime that it has been punished by death. What makes this crime seem worse than many other serious crimes?

### *Challenging the Text*

9. Why do you think Stevenson shifts the **point of view** in this section? Does this switch make the story harder to read? If so, what other solution might Stevenson have tried?

# Chapters 13–21 *(continued)*

## *Treasure Island*

# Choices: Building Your Portfolio

**SMALL GROUP DISCUSSION**

## Theme Hunt
Work with a few classmates to choose one of the novel's major **themes:** "The Struggle Between Two Opposing Forces," "From Innocence to Maturity," or "The Power of Greed." Then, take turns, in round-robin fashion, giving examples from this section of the text that illustrate that theme. When you have named all the examples you can, try a "hunt" on another theme.

**PANEL DISCUSSION**

## Critics' Corner
Critics have had different things to say about the violence in *Treasure Island.* Some dislike it. Others feel that it is true to life and that Stevenson handles it acceptably. What do you think? Organize a panel discussion with a group of classmates. Consider these questions: Is the violence necessary or justified? Does Stevenson handle it appropriately? How does the novel's violence compare to that which is found today in novels, on television, and in movies?

**SKETCH**

## Sketching Subject
Choose one of Stevenson's detailed **descriptions,** such as his description of the stockade and block-house or of the island itself. Make a detailed sketch of the subject, following Stevenson's description as closely as possible.

**CREATIVE WRITING**

## Good Friends Can Be Real Characters
Long John Silver is one of the most intriguing, memorable **characters** in literature. He isn't entirely a work of fiction, though; he is modeled on Stevenson's good friend William E. Henley. Choose a good friend of yours and imagine how you might cast him or her as a character in a story or novel. Write a brief character sketch of your friend as a fictional character.

## Consider This . . .
*Then it was that there came into my head the first of the mad notions that contributed so much to save our lives.*

When Jim sneaks ashore with the pirates, it turns out to be a good idea—but is this any way for a crew member to act? What do you think?

### *Writing Follow-up: Analyzing Effects*

Consider the effects of Jim's going ashore and contrast them to the effects of what might have happened had Jim stayed on board ship.

### Novel Notes

Use **Novel Notes, Issue 4**

- to find out more about some of the topics and themes in Chapters 13–21
- to get ideas for writing activities and other projects related to *Treasure Island*

Study Guide | **19**

# Chapters 22–27

## Treasure Island

## Making Meanings

### First Thoughts

1. Do you agree with Jim's decision to sneak off from his friends?

### Shaping Interpretations

2. In Chapter 23, Jim talks about being favored by "fortune." In your opinion, how much of Jim's success is a matter of "fortune"? How much is the result of his own actions?

3. How does Jim's recovery of the *Hispaniola* illustrate the **theme** of "The Struggle Between Two Opposing Forces"? What does it say about that theme?

> **READING CHECK**
>
> a. What does Dr. Livesey do after the battle?
> b. Describe what happens after Jim cuts the anchor of the *Hispaniola*.
> c. What does Jim do when he sees the *Hispaniola* adrift the next morning?
> d. Aboard the ship, what agreement do Jim and Hands make with each other, and why?
> e. What does Jim suspect when he approaches the stockade? Why? What makes him change his mind?

4. At the end of Chapter 27, Jim returns from retaking the *Hispaniola*, only to fall into the hands of the pirates. Why is this an appropriate place for the end of Part Five? How does this surprise help shape the **plot** of the story?

### Connecting with the Text

5. Think about the struggle between Jim and Hands. How does it compare with other such action scenes that you have read about or seen in a movie or in a television program?

### Extending the Text

6. Throughout the story so far, Jim has trusted his instincts—and has done well. Do you think that "you should trust your instincts" is an idea that most people believe?

### Challenging the Text

7. Long John Silver may be the most interesting, best-drawn **character** in the novel. If you had written *Treasure Island,* would you have made a villain that interesting? Why or why not?

# Chapters 22–27 *(continued)*

*Treasure Island*

# Choices: Building Your Portfolio

### ART

## Sketch Shuffle

With several classmates, divide this section into as many "pieces" as there are people in your group. Have each person choose the main event in his or her "piece" and make a sketch of the action. Each sketch should also include a one-sentence caption that describes what is happening. As a group, review the sketches. Put them in order, numbering them on the back. Then, shuffle the sketches and exchange them with the sketches that another group has made. Looking only at the front of each sketch, can you put the other group's sketches in the right order?

### PHONE CALL

## Reviewing the Situation

Imagine that Jim and Dr. Livesey have cellular phones. Jim is already at sea when Livesey discovers that he is gone, so Livesey phones him. With a partner, discuss the situation. Imagine what Livesey might say. (For example, how well would he understand Jim's reason for leaving? How might he try to get Jim to come back?) Imagine Jim's answers, too. If you wish, try acting out the conversation you have discussed.

### CROSSWORD

## Puzzle It Out

Choose a topic or **theme** and create a crossword puzzle or word search using words from Chapters 22–27. For example, you might create a crossword puzzle using nautical terms, terms referring to the "Struggle Between Two Opposing Forces" theme, or terms relating to another theme. Photocopy your puzzle to share with classmates.

### CREATIVE WRITING

## Headline News!

Imagine that you are a newspaper reporter. Your editor in chief has heard a rumor about the expedition to Treasure Island and has sent you to investigate and to write up a report. You arrive just as Jim Hawkins steps off the recaptured *Hispaniola,* so you interview him on the spot. Write your news report. If you wish, act it out for the class, or add it to your writing portfolio.

## *Consider This . . .*

*It was a smile that had in it something both of pain and weakness—a haggard, old man's smile; but there was, besides that, a grain of derision, a shadow of treachery, in his expression as he craftily watched, and watched, and watched me at my work.*

Jim has no place to run to escape Israel Hands. He knows that violence will erupt, but he doesn't know when. If you were Jim, how would you feel at this moment? What advice might you give him?

### *Writing Follow-up: Solving Problems*

Describe the situation Jim faces and provide solutions to his problem.

---

### Novel Notes

Use **Novel Notes, Issue 5**

- to find out more about some of the topics and themes in Chapters 22–27
- to get ideas for writing activities and other projects related to *Treasure Island*

Study Guide | 21

# Chapters 28–34

*Treasure Island*

## Making Meanings

### First Thoughts

1. Respond to the final chapters of *Treasure Island* by completing these sentences.

   - I thought the treasure would be found by . . .
   - I thought that, in the end, Long John Silver would . . .
   - I was most surprised by . . .

### Shaping Interpretations

2. After Jim walks into the pirate stronghold, Silver begins to play what Hawkins describes as a "remarkable game." What is this "game," and why is it "remarkable"?

3. The idea of duty has appeared throughout the novel. What "duties" do **characters** perform in these final chapters?

4. Hawkins wonders why Dr. Livesey handed the stockade and the treasure map to the pirates. How does Jim's confusion affect you, as a reader?

5. Why do you think Stevenson allows Long John Silver to escape at the end?

### Connecting with the Text

6. When Jim is captured by the pirates, he promises Silver that he won't run away. When Dr. Livesey urges him to escape, Jim remains true to his promise. How hard do you think it is for him to keep his word? What would you have done?

### Extending the Text

7. According to a common proverb, "A fool and his money are soon parted." Reread the last few paragraphs of *Treasure Island*. Whom would this proverb describe as foolish? Why?

### Challenging the Text

8. Some critics have complained that the ending of *Treasure Island* is weak. Do you like the ending? Why or why not?

---

**READING CHECK**

a. What do the pirates decide in their council at the blockhouse, and why?

b. What sound frightens the pirates during their search for the treasure? What do they think it is at first? What do they come to realize about it?

c. Describe what happens at the site of the buried treasure.

d. Where is the treasure? What do Jim and his companions do with it?

# Chapters 28–34 (continued)

## Treasure Island

# Choices: Building Your Portfolio

**DISCUSSION**

## The Big Wrap-Up

Have your teacher divide your class into seven groups. Each group should take one of the last seven chapters of *Treasure Island*. In your group, help each other to become "experts" on your chapter. Read the chapter to each other. Discuss the **characters,** the **dialogue,** and the important **themes** or ideas. Finally, list five points that you want other people to understand about your chapter. Then, have your teacher reorganize the class into new groups, with each group having at least one representative from each of the "chapter" groups. Share your "expert" thoughts on your chapter, and listen to the thoughts from other group members about their chapters.

**SKETCH/DESCRIPTION**

## Walking Around in Someone Else's Shoes

Try this experiment: Imagine yourself as any one of the **characters** in these chapters, and then choose one moment in the **plot.** Close your eyes and think about what has happened to you during this voyage. Now, in the role of that character, open your eyes. Quickly jot down a description or make a rough sketch of the scene before your eyes. How does this experiment help you understand that character better?

**CREATIVE WRITING**

## Who Says?

Most of *Treasure Island* is told from the **point of view** of Jim Hawkins. How would the story be different if someone else told the story? Select a scene to retell. For example, how would Ben Gunn tell about the surprise of the pirates? How would Long John Silver narrate the episode of hunting for the treasure? Try to sound like the **character** you are pretending to be; then, write your story. Read it to a group of classmates.

## Consider This . . .

*It went to all our hearts, I think, to leave them in that wretched state; but we could not risk another mutiny; and to take them home for the gibbet would have been a cruel sort of kindness.*

After all he has been through, Jim still feels somewhat sorry for the pirates who are being marooned on Treasure Island. If you were in Jim's position, how would you have described your feelings at this moment? Why?

### *Writing Follow-up: Pesuading*

Should the pirates be marooned, or should they suffer a different fate? Take a stand and persuade the captain. Explain your position.

## Novel Notes

Use **Novel Notes, Issue 6**

- to find out more about the topics and themes in Chapters 28–34
- to get ideas for writing activities and other projects related to *Treasure Island*

Study Guide | **23**

# Novel Projects

*Treasure Island*

## Cross-Curricular Connections

**SOCIAL STUDIES**

### Why Piracy?
Why did some sailors of the 1600s and 1700s turn to piracy? Were they just after quick wealth? Did they seek adventure? Were they in search of a freedom they could not find anywhere else? Investigate the answers to these questions, and come up with several explanations for the reasons that people became pirates. Present your findings in the form of several interviews or a panel discussion.

**MATHEMATICS**

### The Cost of Piracy
Find out how much treasure—and what kind of treasure—was plundered by pirates. You could choose several pirates (such as Captain Kidd, Blackbeard, and Sir Henry Morgan) and make a study of the worth of the treasure the pirates captured. Alternatively, you could choose a single year or period and investigate the amount of shipping plundered by pirates during that time. Present the information on a chart or graph. You might also try converting the worth of the pirate treasure to present-day prices.

**GEOGRAPHY**

### The Pirate World
Piracy was an international enterprise. Prepare a bulletin-board display that has a world map at its center. Use pushpins to mark the locations of some of the most famous pirate activity (including the Caribbean and the Far East). Then, use yarn or string to lead from the pushpins to index cards upon which you have summarized the facts about each site.

**ART**

### Artful Treasures
Treasure hunters of both the past and the present have been interested in more than just gold coins. Form a small group, and look for information about jewelry, statues, and other artistic crafts that have been part of treasure-troves. You might also consider information about sunken ships and lost mines. Draw or paint pictures of some art objects that you would like to see in a "Treasures Lost and Found" display at an art gallery.

**TECHNOLOGY**

### High-Tech Piracy
In recent years the word *piracy* has taken on new meaning in terms of copyright violation—in book publishing, music recording, and software distribution. Conduct research so you can summarize the problem and explain when people may become "unintentional pirates" by mishandling copyrighted materials.

**SCIENCE**

### Navigating the World
Long John Silver wants Captain Smollett to command the *Hispaniola* as long as possible because Smollett is the only one on board who can navigate a course at sea. Find out how difficult this job is by reading and reporting on the science of navigation during the 1700s. Make diagrams and illustrations to help explain the information; in addition, you may try demonstrating some navigational methods.

# Novel Projects (continued)

## Treasure Island

# Multimedia and Internet Connections

*NOTE: Check with your teacher about school policies on accessing Internet sites. If a Web site named here is not available, use key words to locate a similar site.*

**FILM: REVIEW**

## Comparing Versions

A number of tellings of *Treasure Island* exist. Some attempt to tell Stevenson's tale accurately; others give it a modern or comic "spin." View one or more of these films and write a review that compares the film version to the novel. You might respond to these questions:

- How closely does the film follow the plot of the novel?
- Are the characters true to the novel?
- How does the film handle the violence found in the novel?
- Is the film superior to the novel in any way? Explain.

**RADIO: RADIO SCRIPT**

## "And Last" . . . or Is It?

*Treasure Island* ends without answering three interesting questions: (1) What happens to the three pirates marooned on the island? (2) What becomes of Silver? and (3) What does Jim go on to do with his life? Select one of these questions and write a radio script that could answer it. Include cues for sound effects and music. If possible, cast the show, select techincians, rehearse, and record the script. Play the program for the class.

**TELEVISION: NEWS MAGAZINE**

## Special Report

Think of several television programs with a news-magazine format. Most of their stories run five to ten minutes in length and the reporting often focuses on the "human interest" aspect of the news. Form a group and prepare (and videotape, if possible) a segment for a television news-magazine about the voyage to recover Captain Flint's buried treasure. Have one member of the group be the director. Have another be the camera operator. The rest of the group should take various parts: the reporter, the news anchor, or one of the story characters. The reporter could interview Jim, Dr. Livesey, Squire Trelawney, Captain Smollett, and perhaps Long John Silver. The reporter might also interview a spokesperson from the British Admiralty to learn the official response to the mutiny and to the decision to maroon the last three pirates on Treasure Island.

**INTERNET: WRITING**

## Online Book Review

Write and publish a review of *Treasure Island* on the Internet. Remember that an online review should fulfill all the requirements expected of a traditional review—careful organization, clear ideas, and logical support. You might consider publishing at the following Web site or on a Web site sponsored by a local bookstore.

- http://www.amazon.com

Study Guide

# Novel Projects (continued)

## Treasure Island

**INTERNET: RESEARCH**

### "Netting" the Answer

Who were the pirates? Is Stevenson's portrayal of pirates accurate? Were pirates really bold enough to walk the streets of English cities? Who in the world of piracy were Mary Read and Anne Bonny? Where might someone look for real buried treasure? Think of other questions about pirates. Then, try to find the answers on the Internet. You may wish to browse, or you may prefer to use the following Web site as a starting point:

- Ports O' Call On the Internet
  http://www.discover.net/~nqgiven/ports.htm

Share your search experiences and the answers you find.

**INTERNET: GAMES**

### Pirate Play

Robert Louis Stevenson helped to make the quest for pirate gold a favorite fantasy. Look on the Internet for games or reviews of games that deal with pirates or a search for lost treasure. These three Web sites are just a few of the game forums that allow topical searches and software downloads.

- Gamecenter
  http://www.gamecenter.com

- Happy Puppy
  http://www.happypuppy.com

- Jumbo! The Games Channel
  http://www.jumbo.com/pages/games

In what ways do these games compare to the events found in *Treasure Island*? Share your findings.

# Exploring the Connections

## Making Meanings
### The Mildenhall Treasure

*Novel Notes*
See **Issue 7**

1. Suppose that you had found the treasure. What would you have done with it?
2. Look again at Dahl's **description** of Butcher early in the story. How does this early description of Butcher help you understand him later?
3. When Butcher tells his wife about his discovery, she observes that Ford is a "foxy one." Butcher replies that Ford was "pretty excited about it all." They both feel suspicious about Ford. Why do you think that they do not ask Ford about the treasure later?
4. Jim Hawkins comes across a treasure map in *Treasure Island* and Gordon Butcher discovers treasure. How are these two treasure-hunting **characters** alike? How are they different?
5. Suppose that Butcher had gone to someone like Dr. Livesey instead of to Ford. Would Livesey's reaction have been different from Ford's? Would Butcher have been any happier at the end of the story if Livesey, not Ford, had helped him? Cite details from the story and from *Treasure Island* to support your answer.
6. If you had been on the jury, how would you have decided the case? Was a crime committed? What kind of reward should be awarded, and to whom? Explain your answer.
7. Do you approve of the British law that requires all gold and silver treasure to be turned over to the government? Why or why not?
8. According to the introductory note, Dahl interviewed only Gordon Butcher. He promised Butcher that he "would write a truthful story" about the treasure. In your opinion, could Dahl "write a truthful story" after interviewing just one person? Should he have tried harder to interview Ford, Dr. Fawcett, or officials at the British Museum? Explain.

> **READING CHECK**
> a. What is the Mildenhall treasure?
> b. Where and how does Gordon Butcher discover it?
> c. How does Ford take possession of the treasure?
> d. What finally happens to the treasure?

Study Guide | **27**

# Exploring the Connections (continued)

## Making Meanings

### "We Found It! We Found It!"

*Novel Notes*
See **Issue 7**

1. How would you have reacted when you found out that government officials wanted the treasure?
2. What does Amy Wilentz, the writer of the article, want us to know about Fisher's personality? Cite details to support your answer.
3. Did Fisher have the same reasons for looking for the *Atocha* that Jim Hawkins and the crew of the *Hispaniola* had for their search? Explain.
4. What **themes,** or main ideas, do the facts in this article suggest? Name one fact that supports each theme.
5. Mel Fisher gave up poultry farming to pursue his dream. What dreams do you want to pursue?

**READING CHECK**

a. In 1985, what was the estimated value of the *Atocha* treasure?
b. What "false lead" kept Fisher looking in the wrong place?
c. Who died during the treasure hunt?
d. How did Fisher find the treasure?

### Tiger Moran's Loot

*Novel Notes*
See **Issue 7**

1. Would you want to team up with this group to go in search of treasure? Why or why not?
2. From the clues in this selection, what do you know about Gramps?
3. Gramps, Sam, and the others speak informally. Give two examples of informal speech in this selection. Then describe how the use of informal speech helps you imagine this **scene** taking place.
4. Compare this group of present-day treasure hunters with the group that you met in *Treasure Island*.
5. Do you think that real-life gangsters probably hid great sums of money before they died? Why or why not?

**READING CHECK**

a. In the past, how did Sudden Sam and Slick Jones know each other?
b. Why have Gramps and the young people come to see Sam?

# Exploring the Connections (continued)

## Making Meanings

*Return to the* **Titanic**

*Novel Notes*
See **Issue 8**

1. As you read the **description** of the wreck, what were your reactions? Explain.

2. The explorers aboard the *Alvin* must leave the Grand Staircase because of their schedule. Why do the explorers need to follow a schedule so closely?

3. On the first descent, the *Alvin* is set down upon the deck of the *Titanic*. Ballard worries whether the subdecking will hold. What might have been the result if the deck had collapsed under the weight of the sub?

4. What kind of treasure is Ballard seeking? How does it compare to the treasure sought by Jim Hawkins and Long John Silver?

5. Even before you start reading, you know the outcome: Ballard will find the *Titanic*. How, then, does he keep **suspense** in his story? That is, how does he make you feel uncertain or anxious about what will happen next?

6. Ballard compares the descent to the bottom of the ocean in the *Alvin* to "astronauts landing on a distant planet." Would you have volunteered for a ride to the bottom of the ocean in the *Alvin?* Why or why not?

7. Visiting the *Titanic* was an expensive, risky adventure. Do you think that visiting sunken ships like the *Titanic* is important? Why or why not?

> **READING CHECK**
> a. How do the scientists reach the *Titanic*?
> b. What do the scientists use to explore the inside of the Grand Staircase?
> c. What kinds of items from the *Titanic* do they find?

Study Guide | 29

# Novel Notes

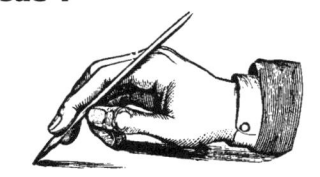

**Issue 1**

## *Introducing* TREASURE ISLAND

### Piracy—Once It Was Legal

Sea captains who commanded their own armed ships were hired during wartime by various governments to attack their enemies' shipping. Because these "privateers" were allowed to keep the cargo of the ships they captured, theirs was a profitable business during wartime and a hard-to-break habit when a war was over.

A Rhode Island privateer named Thomas Tew was hired by the English in the late 1600s to attack Spanish and French ships. Then England and Spain made peace, and Tew found that French ships were carrying so little treasure that it was hardly worth the trouble to board them.

Tew and some backers hatched a plan: Papers from the governor of Bermuda would authorize Tew to attack "legally" a French trading post on the west coast of Africa. Instead, he would head for India and the riches of the Great Mogul. The plan worked. Tew quickly captured a Mogul ship with more than £100,000 in gold and silver coin. Privateering had become piracy. Word of the potential riches spread, other privateers were fast to follow, and the golden age of piracy had begun.

> **FOR YOUR READER'S LOG**
> Think about this sentence:
> *If I could talk to Robert Louis Stevenson, I would ask him. . . .*
> Write the sentence in your Reader's Log. Add questions as you read the novel.

## ROGUES' GALLERY
### MEN YOU WOULDN'T WANT TO MEET ON THE WATER

**Captain William Kidd**

Kidd stole so much treasure—and hid it so well—that some of it has never been found. A New York captain of a merchant ship, Kidd was hired by the English to capture pirates. He quickly found piracy to his liking and in a three-year voyage accumulated enormous wealth. When he returned to New York in 1701, the English hanged him.

**Blackbeard**

His name was Edward Teach, but he was called Blackbeard because of his long black beard, which he braided into plaits and tied with ribbons. He carried three pistols, and in battle he stuck long, lighted matches under his hat to create a frame of fire around his face. Reputedly, he had fourteen wives. In 1717 and 1718, he terrorized the Carolina and Virginia coasts, blockading the port of Charleston and kidnapping citizens for ransom. He was stopped in a battle with forces from Virginia and Carolina, and he died on November 21, 1718, with twenty-five wounds on his body.

**Sir Henry Morgan**

Morgan is a success story. He began as a foot soldier with an English expedition to the West Indies in 1655. By 1656, he had become a privateer, with the blessings of the Jamaican governor, to defend the English against Spain. Morgan was quite successful, at one time leading two thousand men and thirty-eight ships in an attack on Panama. A new Jamaican governor, however, arrested Morgan for piracy and sent him to England for trial. Instead of punishing him, King Charles II knighted Morgan and sent him back to Jamaica—as governor!

Treasure Island

# Novel Notes

**Issue 2**

## TREASURE ISLAND Chapters 1–6

### Sailors Warned: Beware the Dry Tortugas

The Dry Tortugas are eight islands and reefs that extend into the Gulf of Mexico about 110 kilometers west of the Florida Keys. Their combination of shallow waters and pirate lairs have meant disaster for hundreds of ships that strayed off course or were swept to the Tortugas by storms. Since 1650, more than 250 ships have sunk in these waters.

> **FOR YOUR READER'S LOG**
>
> Suppose that you live near a port city during the 1700s. What kind of people would you expect to meet there? As you read these first chapters, jot down some notes about the characters whom Stevenson introduces.

---

**STURDY SEA CHESTS AVAILABLE:**
PRICED TO FIT A SAILOR'S BUDGET
Come to Davy Jones's Discount Locker for All Your Sailing Needs

Our sea chests are large, sturdy, and easy to carry from ship to shore to ship. On board, they double as chair, closet, chest of drawers, and a stand for holding your day's supply of water.

---

### SPOTLIGHT ON *TREASURE ISLAND*
### Lots of Loot

In *Treasure Island,* the items in Billy Bones's sea chest were chosen by the writer's father, who was fascinated by the story his son was creating. Stevenson wrote,

> When the time came for Billy Bones's chest to be ransacked, he must have spent the better part of a day preparing, on the back of a legal envelope, an inventory of its contents, which I exactly followed.

---

## The Word PLACE

### Pirate Plunder

"... the coins were of all countries and sizes—doubloons and louis d'ors, and guineas, and pieces of eight ..."

**Piece of eight:** A Spanish peso that corresponded to the United States dollar. It was worth eight reals (Spanish coins) and had an *8* stamped on it.

**Doubloon:** This Spanish coin was used until the 1800s. It was worth about sixteen silver dollars.

**Louis d'or:** Any of the gold coins minted during the reigns of the French kings from Louis XIII through Louis XVI—from 1610 to 1792.

**Guinea:** An English coin used between 1663 and 1813.

Study Guide  31

# Novel Notes

**Issue 3**

## TREASURE ISLAND Chapters 7–12

## Schooner, the Ship of Choice

A beautiful and practical ship, the schooner was a favorite sailing ship from the 1600s well into the late 1800s. The rigging of the ship was simple enough to be managed by a small crew. Schooners of the 1700s usually had two masts, sharp bows, and square sterns. The *Hispaniola* was a schooner.

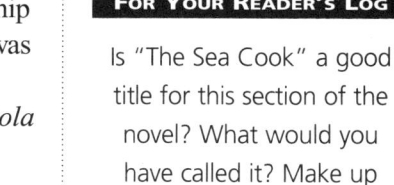

### FOR YOUR READER'S LOG

Is "The Sea Cook" a good title for this section of the novel? What would you have called it? Make up your own alternate titles for each section of the book.

## Music to Sail By

A chantey, or song sailors sang to help them work, provided a rhythm for moves that had to be made at the same time. A chantey for hoisting the topsail, for example, was a yo-HEAVE-ho. Sailors made up different chanteys for different chores.

In a sailor's free time, there was little to do, and voyages could last for months or years. Singing passed time and expressed feelings: a melancholy ballad when you were lonely, a sad lament when you lost a mate to the storm. Singing—if you were a sailor—was as much a part of your life as your sea chest.

## ASK *the Professor*

**Dear Dr. I. Knoweverything,**

*My grandmother says her parrot is sixty years old and will probably live forever. Will I really have to listen to this thing squawk for the rest of my life?*

—**Apprehensive in Alabama**

**Dear Apprehensive,**

With that attitude, you're missing out on some interesting stuff. Yes, parrots can have very long lives, the longest of any domesticated animal, as a matter of fact, and they are amazingly intelligent and sociable. They can mimic human speech right down to tone of voice, and when they figure out how to call the dog. . . . Well, they've driven some canines almost nuts. Some people think that parrots know what they're saying, but this theory is still controversial.

In the wild, they live in flocks, where they chatter away to one another. When they're taken away from the flock and made into pets, they focus their social lives toward the humans around them.

People discovered the fun of having parrots around in the quite distant past; in fact, they have been domesticated longer than almost any other animal.

Your grandmother's parrot probably won't live past seventy or eighty, so get to know it now. You have some surprises coming up!

32 | *Treasure Island*

# Novel Notes

**Issue 4**

## TREASURE ISLAND Chapters 13–21

## Who's in Charge Here?

Discipline and order were essential on a pirate ship.

The **captain** was the man in charge. A pirate captain got his position and held it through his own power and persuasion. On some pirate ships, however, he was elected and exercised his position mainly during battles.

The **mate** was second in command to the captain. (Captain Flint's mate was Billy Bones.)

The **quartermaster** on a pirate ship was almost equal to the captain in power. He enforced the ship's laws, and when the ship was in battle, he usually served as the helmsman or pilot. (Long John Silver was Captain Flint's quartermaster.)

The **coxswain** was the pilot, the officer who steered the ship. (Israel Hands was the coxswain on the *Hispaniola*.)

The **boatswain** was in charge of the ship's maintenance and supplies. (Job Anderson was the *Hispaniola's* boatswain.)

As the name suggests, the **gunner** was in charge of the cannon. (Israel Hands was Flint's gunner.)

**FOR YOUR READER'S LOG**

Would you have behaved in the same way Jim did? Explain.

### Stevenson Finds Characters in Many Sources

**Israel Hands,** the *Hispaniola's* coxswain and gunner, was, in real life, a good mate of the infamous Blackbeard. Blackbeard turned over command of one captured ship to Hands. Later, Hands became a well-known London beggar.

Stevenson modeled **Long John Silver** on his good friend William E. Henley. In creating the character, Stevenson said he decided to "take an admired friend of mine . . . to deprive him of all his finer qualities and higher graces of temperament, to leave him with nothing but his strength, his courage, and his quickness, and his magnificent geniality."

## Last Flag Seen by Pirates' Victims

A white skull and crossbones on a black field, flying from a top mast, brought fear to any ship that saw it approaching. It was the Jolly Roger—a pirate flag. Pirates flew it to identify themselves to each other and to their prey—merchant ships of any nation.

Some of the first pirate flags were blood red with various sinister symbols such as a skeleton, an arm and cutlass, or an hourglass. By the 1690s, though, most pirates flew the Jolly Roger and personalized it with their own design. Enemy to the Jolly Roger was the Union Jack, the common name for the national flag of Great Britain. When Captain Smollett "ran up the colors," he raised the Union Jack.

Study Guide  **33**

# Novel Notes

**Issue 5**

## TREASURE ISLAND Chapters 22–27

### What's Cookin'
#### MENU FOR HISPANIOLA

**Monday**

**Salt horse:** All you can eat, mates, of our matchless dried beef packed in salt—hard and red. I soak it a day so I can cook with it. **Reminder:** A prize for the sailor who carves the best item from salt horse.

**hardtack:** Many of you have asked for my recipe; here it is: Mix flour, salt, and a little water into a small cake; bake for two to three hours until it is completely dry and hard as a rock; stays fresh indefinitely.

**Tuesday, Wednesday, Thursday**

**Salt horse, hardtack** (You know what you can do about this, boys! If you're too lazy to catch some fish for your old Cookie, you can keep chewing on salt horse.)

**Friday**

**Delightful Duff** made from flour, lard, yeast, finely chopped salt horse (from the pork barrel), and molasses

**Saturday PLUS**

PORT CALL!! All the mangoes and bananas we can eat, boys.

### FOR YOUR READER'S LOG

If you could have a conversation with Jim, what would you like to tell him or ask him? As ideas come to mind, note them in your Reader's Log.

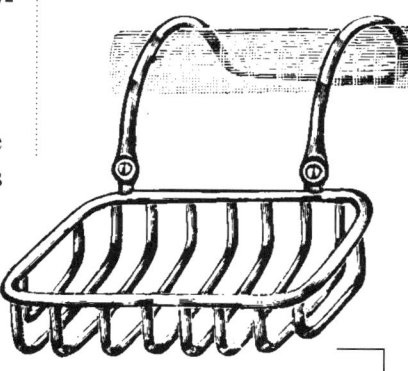

---

## Ask the Professor

**Dear Dr. I. Knoweverything,**

*My brother loves to sail and hates to bathe. He thinks he'd have a great life as a pirate. Would he?*

—Sister in Springfield

**Dear Sister,**

Your brother is in for a rude awakening. Pirates in movies and stories usually appear to have a totally carefree life with little work and no worries. Their captain is handsome and bold, and they're always singing. In fact, pirates were probably fairly miserable. They often fought among themselves, and many died from wounds or diseases. Others were shot or captured and jailed or executed. Some were marooned by their own shipmates. Depending partly on how much power the captain had, the men on board slept when and where they wanted and worked as little as possible. As a result, pirate ships were a mess, filthy and in bad repair. However, when their own ships were no longer seaworthy, they simply captured another one and took it over.

Tell your brother it's time to read a little nonfiction!

---

## The Word PLACE

### Buccaneer

*Buccaneer* is another name for pirate. It has come a long way from the French word *boucanier*—"smoker of meat."

English and French refugees on the Caribbean island of Hispaniola were herders and prepared their meat by smoking it on open wooden frames. The Spanish, who claimed the island, considered the boucaniers to be illegal settlers and chased them from the island. The boucaniers settled on the island of Tortuga and used it as a base for revenge, raiding Spanish towns and ships. Tortuga eventually became a haven for buccaneers from all over the world.

---

34 | Treasure Island

# Novel Notes

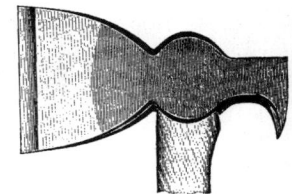

**Issue 6**

## TREASURE ISLAND Chapters 28–34

## Pirates Claim Democratic Society

Possibly because they had been abused by tyrannical captains in their lives as sailors, pirates believed they were equal and that their ship belonged to all of them. Many pirate crews made their own rules and decided together when and whom to attack, where to anchor, and how to divide the plunder. They elected their own captains, and they replaced a captain when he made decisions they didn't like. Only during battle did the captain rule unchallenged. When a sailor joined a pirate crew, he had to swear on either a Bible or an ax that he would obey the ship's laws. If a law was broken, the crew tried the offender, decided his guilt, and decreed his punishment. Every pirate had one vote, regardless of rank.

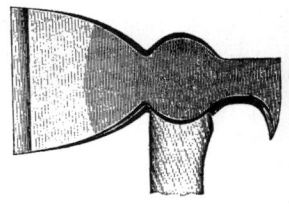

> **FOR YOUR READER'S LOG**
>
> Have events in *Treasure Island* been turning out as you expected? As you read this section, make a note about each unexpected turn of events, or make a sketch to represent it.

## Marooning: Is It a Death Sentence?

Pirates had their own special punishment for shipmates who broke their code. The pirates would row the offender to a deserted island and abandon him there to fend for himself. Some of these islands were only small bits of sand in midocean; they rarely had food or fresh water. In fact, some of the islands were under water at high tide. Since marooning usually meant death—often a slow and painful one of thirst and starvation—it was usually reserved for traitors.

## ASK the Professor

**Dear Dr. I. Knoweverything,**

*Are there still chests of pirate gold buried on remote islands? I'd sure go for that gold!*

—Wishful in Wisconsin

**Dear Wishful,**

Most pirates spent their treasure instead of burying it. Nevertheless, legends of buried treasure persist. Captain Kidd's ship, for example, is said to have been loaded with treasure worth £100,000, or roughly $2,000,000. When Kidd was captured, only a small portion of his treasure was found. Later, £50 thought to be pirate loot was found buried on Gardiners Island near Long Island, New York. Where is the rest? Treasure hunters have searched for more than three hundred years with very little success, but that fact seems not to have discouraged them.

Dream on, or do some real research, and come up with some reasonable hypotheses about where the plunder is buried. Remember, too, that technology is always changing. Maybe you'll be the one to put it all together. If you do, be sure to write back.

Study Guide | 35

# Novel Notes

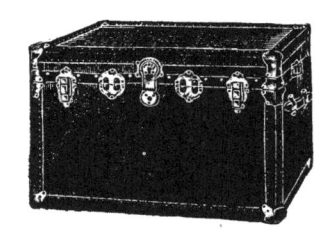

**Issue 7**

## TREASURE ISLAND Connections

### Finders Keepers? If Only!

Many people who have spent years of their lives and most of their money searching for treasure have had to turn over much of their hard-won loot. The British government, for instance, claims all gold and silver treasure found on its soil. Other countries have similar laws. Moreover, governments are not the only claimants; historical preservation societies, ship owners, and insurance companies all insist that certain kinds of found treasure should be theirs. The ultimate right of ownership is usually decided in the courts. As a result, a treasure hunter may spend years searching for treasure and then years fighting to keep it.

### Connections

- **The Mildenhall Treasure**
- **"We Found It! We Found It!"**
- **Tiger Moran's Loot**

## *The Treasure Hunters*

**Jack Harbeston** and his firm found the *Santa Margarita*—and its $200 million in gold—in the western Pacific.

**Paul Tidwell** discovered a Japanese submarine that had been torpedoed and sunk during World War II. It carried two tons of gold, worth at least $24 million.

**Steve Libert** has spent years searching Lake Michigan for the *Poverty Island,* a ship that supposedly went down with $400 million in gold aboard. Pirates sank the ship in the 1860s.

In 1937, **Milton "Doc" Noss** claimed to have found 16,000 bars of Spanish gold in a New Mexico cave. While trying to remove the gold, he accidentally dynamited the cave entrance shut! Undaunted, Noss's heirs continue to search for the gold.

**FOR YOUR READER'S LOG**

Who "owns" a treasure that someone discovers? Imagine how the people that you are reading about might answer the question. Write your ideas in your Reader's Log.

## Treasure Writers

**Roald Dahl** As a teenager, Dahl (1916–1990) wanted a life of adventure. After he finished school, he worked for an oil company in Africa. He loved the "roasting heat and the crocodiles and the snakes and the long safaris up-country." His writing career began by accident. A writer interviewed Dahl for an article. The writer, however, was too busy eating during the interview to take notes, so Dahl took them instead. When the writer submitted them under Dahl's name to the *Saturday Evening Post,* the *Post* paid Dahl $1,000. That got him interested; Dahl went on to write novels, short stories, plays, and nonfiction.

**Walter Dean Myers** Myers (born in 1937) began writing short stories when he was ten, and for many years after, he thought of writing as just an enjoyable hobby. Finally, "I decided that what I wanted to do with myself was to become a writer and live what I imagined would be the life of the writer." He entered a writing contest and won. Since that time, he has written dozens of books for children and young adults.

# Novel Notes

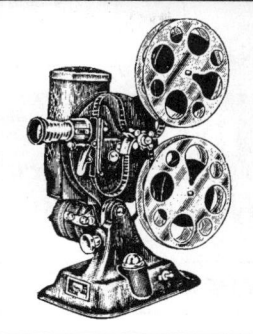

**Issue 8**

## TREASURE ISLAND Connections

### At the Movies with the *Titanic*

Of the many *Titanic* films, these four are particularly worth a view.

***Saved from the Titanic*** (1912) This silent film was first shown on May 14, 1912, just twenty-nine days after the *Titanic* had sunk. Its co-writer was Dorothy Gibson, a *Titanic* survivor. Gibson also stars in the film, wearing the same clothes that she wore when the ship sank.

***Titanic*** (1953) Starring Clifton Webb and Barbara Stanwyck, this Academy Award–winning version focuses on two of the passengers.

***A Night to Remember*** (1958) This respected British film is a dramatized adaptation of Walter Lord's book about the disaster.

***Titanic*** (1997) A love story with impressive visual effects, this blockbuster won eleven Academy Awards, including Best Picture.

### Connections

- **Return to the *Titanic***

### *Titanic* Data

- It was 882 feet long (the length of three football fields).
- Its hull was divided into 16 watertight compartments; even if two flooded, the *Titanic* was to stay afloat.
- The ship had only one set of high powered binoculars. The seamen on watch in the crow's nest weren't allowed to use them.
- At 11:40 P.M. on April 14, 1912, the *Titanic* struck an iceberg. Six of the ship's watertight compartments flooded immediately.
- Two and one half hours later, the ship broke apart and sank.
- There were over 2,000 passengers and crew aboard, but the ship carried enough lifeboats for only half of them. Many boats left the sinking liner only half-filled.
- In all, 1,517 people died in the disaster. Only 705 survived.

**FOR YOUR READER'S LOG**

Why do people risk their lives on expeditions like the one to explore the *Titanic*?

### The Word PLACE

*Liner Lingo*

**bridge:** a ship's control center. All orders emanate from here.
**wheelhouse:** where the steering wheel is located.
**superstructure:** sits on top of the main deck.
**capstan:** looks like an upright spool; rotated manually or mechanically to work the cables wrapped around it.
**davits:** small cranes used to raise and lower lifeboats
**echo sounder:** determines the water's depth by measuring the time it takes for sound waves to bounce off the ocean floor
**sonar:** bounces sound waves off underwater objects to determine their depth and location

Study Guide

Name _____

# Reading Skills and Strategies Worksheet
## Novel Organizer                                                                                             *Treasure Island*

**CHARACTER**

Use the chart below to keep track of the characters in this book. Each time you come across a new character, write the character's name and the number of the page on which the character first appears. Then, jot down a brief description. Add information about the characters as you read. Put a star next to the name of each main character.

| NAME OF CHARACTER | PAGE | DESCRIPTION |
|---|---|---|
|  |  |  |
|  |  |  |
|  |  |  |
|  |  |  |
|  |  |  |
|  |  |  |
|  |  |  |
|  |  |  |
|  |  |  |
|  |  |  |
|  |  |  |
|  |  |  |
|  |  |  |
|  |  |  |

Name _____

# Reading Skills and Strategies Worksheet

**Novel Organizer** *(continued)*  *Treasure Island*

## SETTING

Where and when does this story take place? .............................................................

..............................................................................................................................

..............................................................................................................................

## CONFLICT (Read at least one chapter before you answer.)

What is the biggest problem faced by the main character(s)? ....................................

..............................................................................................................................

..............................................................................................................................

How do you predict it will be resolved? ...................................................................

..............................................................................................................................

..............................................................................................................................

## MAJOR EVENTS

- ..........................................................................................................................
- ..........................................................................................................................
- ..........................................................................................................................
- ..........................................................................................................................
- ..........................................................................................................................

## OUTCOME

How is the main problem resolved? (How accurate was your prediction?) ..................

..............................................................................................................................

..............................................................................................................................

Name _____ Date _____

# Reading Skills and Strategies Worksheet
*Treasure Island*

## Chapters 1–6: Describing Characters

As you enter the world of *Treasure Island,* you quickly meet several **characters.** Keep track of them by completing this chart.

**Next to each character's name, write a physical description of the character and a characterizing action or behavior that you find in Chapters 1–6. Not all characters will be physically described in these chapters. If you wish, expand upon this chart as you continue reading.**

| CHARACTER | PHYSICAL DESCRIPTION | ACTIONS |
|---|---|---|
| Jim Hawkins | | |
| Jim's mother | | |
| Billy Bones | | |
| Black Dog | | |
| Pew | | |
| Dr. Livesey | | |
| Squire Trelawney | | |

**40** | *Treasure Island*

Name _____ Date _____

# Reading Skills and Strategies Worksheet
*Treasure Island*

## Chapters 7–12: Responding to Quotations

Use the following chart to think about this section of *Treasure Island*. In the left-hand column, write interesting quotations from the text. These might be about **characters, plot** details, or **themes**—anything that catches your attention. In the right-hand column, jot down a response to each quotation. You might ask a question about the quotation, describe how it makes you feel, or connect it to other stories that you have read.

| QUOTATION | RESPONSE |
|---|---|
|   |   |
|   |   |
|   |   |
|   |   |
|   |   |
|   |   |
|   |   |
|   |   |
|   |   |

Study Guide | **41**

Name _____ Date _____

# Reading Skills and Strategies Worksheet
*Treasure Island*

## Chapters 13–21: Tracking Plot Details

Exciting events take place in this part of *Treasure Island*. To complicate the **plot,** part of it is told by Jim and part by Dr. Livesey. The events that these two **narrators** tell about happen at the same time. Completing the following diagram will help you organize the details.

**Fill in the boxes with major plot details, in the order in which they happen.**

| The *Hispaniola* is towed into its anchorage at Treasure Island. |
|---|

↓

|   |
|---|

↓            ↓

| **Jim Hawkins's Narration** | **Dr. Livesey's Narration** |
|---|---|
| ↓ | ↓ |
|   |   |
| ↓ | ↓ |
|   |   |
| ↓ | ↓ |
|   |   |

↓            ↓

|   |
|---|

↓

|   |
|---|

**42** | *Treasure Island*

Name _____ Date _____

# Reading Skills and Strategies Worksheet
*Treasure Island*

## Chapters 22–27: Identifying Problems and Solutions

In this section, Jim Hawkins seems to confront one problem after another. Jim is clever, though, and he keeps coming up with solutions.

**Complete the following chart to trace the chief problems he faces and the solutions he finds.**

| PROBLEM | SOLUTION |
|---|---|
| Jim wants to leave stockade but knows Smollett won't allow it. → | |
| Jim prepares to cut hawser but knows it is very tight and will be dangerous if cut. → | |
|  → | |
|  → | |
|  → | |

Study Guide | **43**

Name _____ Date _____

# Reading Skills and Strategies Worksheet
*Treasure Island*

## Chapters 28–34: Analyzing Events

During this final section of *Treasure Island,* Jim Hawkins goes through a series of powerful emotions.

**In the cluster diagrams, summarize an event in each of the chapters listed that causes a particular emotion in Jim.**

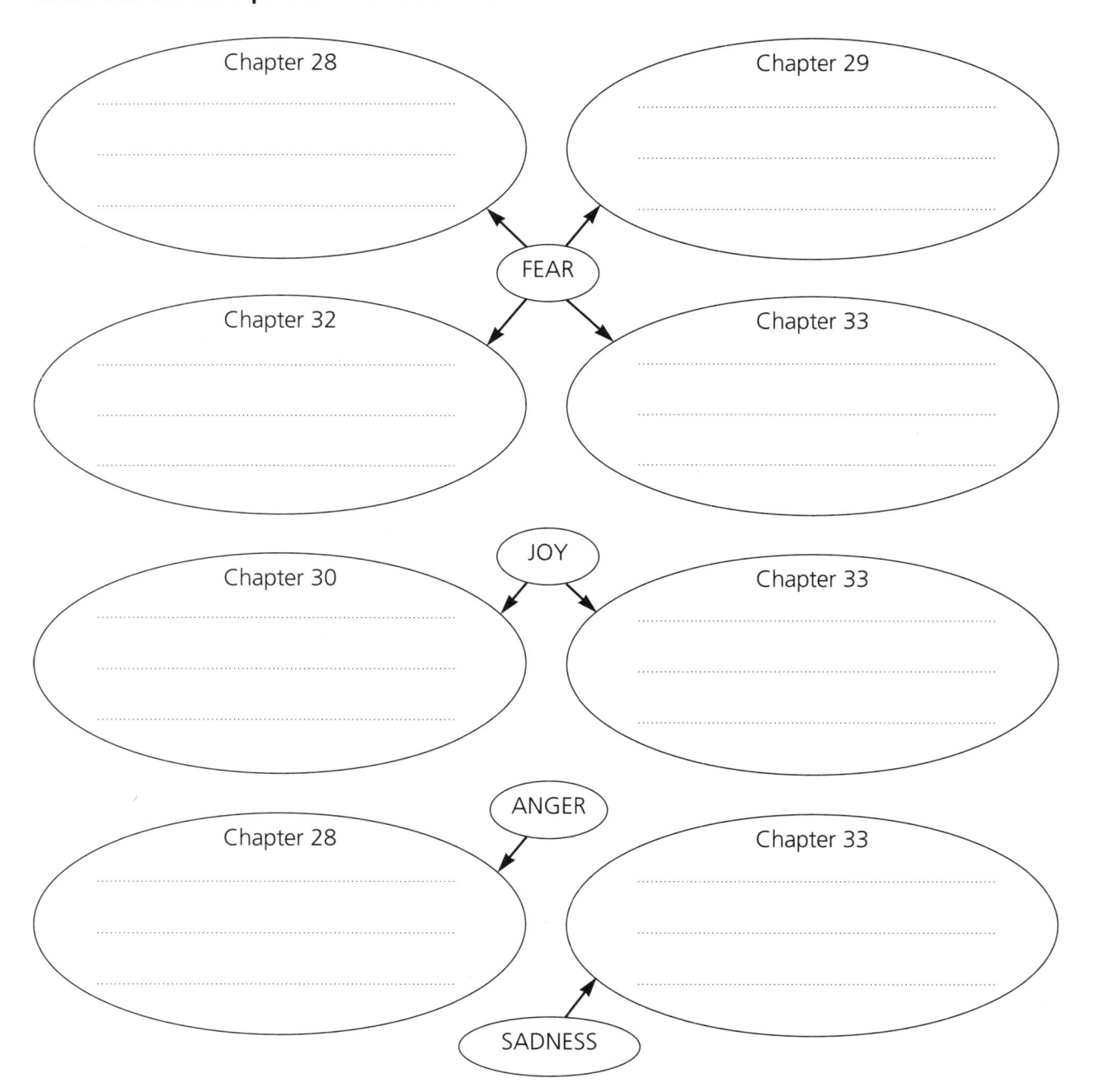

Chapter 28

Chapter 29

FEAR

Chapter 32

Chapter 33

JOY

Chapter 30

Chapter 33

ANGER

Chapter 28

Chapter 33

SADNESS

*Treasure Island*

Name _____ Date _____

# Literary Elements Worksheet

*Treasure Island*

## Plot

**Plot** is the series of related events that make up a story. In *Treasure Island,* as in most stories, the plot includes a **basic situation, complications,** a **climax,** and a **resolution.**

**Chart the plot of *Treasure Island* by completing the following diagram.**

**Climax**

**Resolution**

**Complications**

**Basic Situation**

Study Guide | **45**

Name _____ Date _____

# Literary Elements Worksheet

*Treasure Island*

## Characterization

**Characterization** is the way or ways in which a writer lets us know what a character is like.

**Complete the following diagram to learn more about the ways in which Robert Louis Stevenson characterizes Long John Silver. If you wish, adapt this chart to other characters in *Treasure Island*, too.**

| What others say about him: | What he says: |
|---|---|
|  |  |

### Long John Silver's Characteristics

| What he does: | What he looks like: |
|---|---|
|  |  |

*Treasure Island*

Name _____ Date _____

# Literary Elements Worksheet

*Treasure Island*

## Conflict

A **conflict** is a struggle between opposing characters or opposing forces. It can be either (1) an **external conflict,** in which a character struggles with an outside force, or (2) an **internal conflict,** in which the struggle is within the character. *Treasure Island* has both types of conflict.

**Complete the following chart to analyze some of the conflicts in Stevenson's tale.**

| CHARACTER | SITUATION | INTERNAL OR EXTERNAL | DESCRIPTION OF CONFLICT |
|---|---|---|---|
| Jim's mother | Going through Bones's money | external | |
| Jim | Climbs aboard the drifting *Hispaniola* | | |
| Silver | Handed the black spot | | |
| Jim | | | Jim wants to run but has promised Silver he will remain with the pirates. |
| Captain Smollett | | external | |
| Dr. Livesey | | external | |
| Silver and Jim | | external | They confront the pirates who want to kill both of them. |

Study Guide  **47**

# Glossary

## Treasure Island

- Words are listed by chapter in order of appearance.
- The definition and part of speech are based on the way the word is used in the chapter. For other uses of the word, check a dictionary.
- **Vocabulary Words** are preceded by an asterisk (*) and appear in the **Vocabulary Worksheets**.

### Chapter 1

**connoisseur** *n.:* someone who has good taste or judgment in some field of knowledge

**grog** *n.:* alcoholic beverage

***abominable** *adj.:* awful; horrible

***rebuff** *n.:* blunt rejection

**hamlet** *n.:* small village

***rheumatics** *n.:* painful swelling of the joints

**assizes** *n.:* civil or criminal trials held in British counties

### Chapter 2

**hoar-frost** *n.:* white, frozen dew on a surface

**wanting** *adj.:* lacking

***leer** *n.:* threatening grin

**fancy** *n.:* notion, liking; *v.:* imagine

***sinewy** *adj.:* muscular; powerful

***lancet** *n.:* surgical knife with a short, wide, pointed, double-edged blade

***buccaneer** *n.:* pirate

### Chapter 3

***lee** *adj.:* the side of something that is protected from the wind

**berth** *n.:* sleeping-place; bed

**wrench** *n.:* sudden, forceful twist

### Chapter 4

***detestable** *adj.:* hateful

**whence** *adv.:* where (as in, from what place?)

**whither** *adv.:* where (as in, to what place?)

**wretched** *adj.:* miserable; extremely unhappy

***obstinately** *adv.:* stubbornly

**dispersing** *v.:* breaking up and disappearing

### Chapter 5

**formidable** *adj.:* causing fear and an unwillingness to oppose

**miscreant** *n.:* a bad, evil person

### Chapter 6

***condescending** *adj.:* snobbish

**atrocious** *adj.:* very bad or offensive

***prodigiously** *adv.:* extremely; enormously

**hummock** *n.:* small, rounded hill

### Chapter 7

**brooded** *v.:* thought carefully

***score** *n.:* group of twenty people or objects

***indomitable** *adj.:* unconquerable; not easily defeated

**consort** *n.:* ship that accompanies another

***quays** *n.:* wharves

### Chapter 8

***dexterity** *n.:* skill in using the body

**sheepishly** *adv.:* with embarrassment

***nautical** *adj.:* having to do with the sea

### Chapter 9

**garrison** *n.:* fort

**humbug** *n.:* deceptive person; liar

***galley** *n.:* ship's kitchen

# Glossary (continued)

*Treasure Island*

### Chapter 10

**bustle** *n.:* highly energetic, noisy activity

**wily** *adj.:* skillful in making tricky plans

***trades** *n.:* winds that blow toward the equator all year

### Chapter 11

**christened** *v.:* named (as at the time of launching)

**shiver** *v.:* break into tiny pieces

***derisively** *adv.:* in a manner that shows ridicule or contempt

**square** *adj.:* honest; genuine

### Chapter 12

**duplicity** *n.:* deception or double-dealing

***countenance** *n.:* look of emotion on one's face

**mutiny** *v.:* rebel against authority

**prodigious** *adj.:* great and unusual

### Chapter 13

***qualm** *n.:* feeling of sickness or nausea

**civility** *n.:* politeness; consideration; courtesy

***embark** *v.:* go aboard a boat or ship

### Chapter 14

***undulating** *adj.:* having a wavy or curvy form

**aperture** *n.:* opening

***languor** *n.:* laziness

**warier** *adj.:* more cautious or suspicious

### Chapter 15

**apparition** *n.:* ghostly figure

**supplication** *n.:* the act of making a request or praying

### Chapter 17

***contrived** *adj.:* carefully planned

**provisions** *n.:* supplies of food and other needed items

### Chapter 18

**molestation** *n.:* interference; attack

***sullen** *adj.:* sad; gloomy

### Chapter 20

***placidly** *adv.:* calmly; quietly

**morass** *n.:* swamp

***knoll** *n.:* small hill or mound

**imprecations** *n.:* curses or prayers for destruction of enemies

### Chapter 21

**doldrums** *n.:* equatorial ocean regions noted for a lack of winds

### Chapter 22

**apoplectic** *adj.:* showing signs of a loss of muscular control and/or consciousness due to a ruptured or blocked blood vessel in the brain, as in a stroke

**coracle** *n.:* small frame boat

### Chapter 23

***dolefully** *adv.:* sadly; sorrowfully

**impulsion** *n.:* push

***incessant** *adj.:* unceasing; constant; without ending

**stupor** *n.:* a mental numbness

### Chapter 24

**contrariety** *n.:* lack of agreement or consistency

**disposition** *n.:* placement; positioning

**infallibly** *adv.:* without the possibility of failing

Study Guide | 49

# Glossary (continued)

*Treasure Island*

### Chapter 26

**deception** *n.:* act or practice of misleading or deceiving

**\*subaltern** *n.:* subordinate

**\*dilapidation** *n.:* state of ruin

**grizzled** *adj.:* streaked with gray

### Chapter 27

**dirk** *n.:* dagger with a long, straight blade

**\*subside** *v.:* reduce in intensity; become less

**circumspectly** *adv.:* cautiously

### Chapter 28

**pluckily** *adv.:* with courage and determination

**\*truculently** *adv.:* cruelly or savagely

**\*furtively** *adv.:* secretively; sneakily

### Chapter 29

**incongruous** *adj.:* not being consistent or compatible; inharmonious

**depose** *v.:* overthrow

**\*vehemence** *n.:* great force

### Chapter 30

**admixture** *n.:* something formed by mixing

**pestiferous** *adj.:* filled with disease

**preponderance** *adj.:* superiority or greatness in power

**volubility** *n.:* talkativeness

### Chapter 31

**feasible** *adj.:* able to be accomplished; worthwhile

**ambiguity** *n.:* condition of having two or more possible meanings

**eminence** *n.:* high or lofty place

### Chapter 32

**\*precipices** *n.:* cliffs

**volubly** *adv.:* in a great flow of speech; talkatively

### Chapter 33

**\*insolence** *n.:* disrespect

**\*impostor** *n.:* pretender; one who pretends to be someone else in order to deceive others; fake

**\*obsequious** *adj.:* excessively willing to serve or obey

### Chapter 34

**\*ingratiate** *v.:* bring oneself into another's good graces

**sojourn** *n.:* visit; brief travel

Name _____ Date _____

# Vocabulary Worksheet 1

### Treasure Island: Chapters 1–12

**A. Write the Vocabulary Word from the box that best completes each sentence. (You will not use every word.)**

| obstinately | score | abominable | derisively | indomitable | countenance |
| nautical | lee | buccaneer | trades | prodigiously | condescending |

1. Food from the ship's kitchen was so _____ that the crew became ill.
2. The crew gathered at the door and yelled _____ at the awful cook.
3. Despite the protests, the cook _____ continued laboring over the hot stove.
4. When the mate noticed the horrible grimace on the cook's _____ , he ordered the crew to leave.
5. The ship anchored in the _____ of the island to get out of the wind.
6. The old _____ told many tales of his illegal adventures on the high seas.
7. He had chests full of gold and diamonds and was _____ wealthy.
8. The pirate crew, which was undefeated in battle, was _____.
9. With more _____ training, the young mate will be able to navigate.
10. The _____ were strong and quickly blew the ship home.

**B. In an *analogy,* pairs of words are related in the same way. Complete each of the following analogies with a word from the box. (You will not use every word.)**

| dexterity | detestable | leer | sinewy | rebuff |
| quays | rheumatics | galley | languor | lancet |

11. _____ : lovable :: stingy : generous
12. garage : mechanic :: _____ : cook
13. wharves : _____ :: sailors : seamen
14. rower : strength :: dancer : _____
15. surgeon : _____ :: carpenter : hammer
16. scorn : respect :: acceptance : _____
17. thoughtful : considerate :: _____ : muscular
18. pain : _____ :: laughter : jokes

Study Guide | 51

Name _____  Date _____

# Vocabulary Worksheet 2

*Treasure Island: Chapters 13–34*

**A.** Match each Vocabulary Word in the two left-hand columns with the correct meaning from the two right-hand columns. Write the letter of the definition in the space provided.

| WORD | MEANING |
|---|---|

_____ 1. vehemence     _____ 6. placidly

_____ 2. impostor      _____ 7. incessant

_____ 3. ingratiate    _____ 8. qualm

_____ 4. dilapidation  _____ 9. subside

_____ 5. contrived     _____ 10. obsequious

**a.** excessively willing to serve or obey
**b.** reduce in intensity
**c.** without ending
**d.** carefully planned
**e.** quietly
**f.** state of ruin
**g.** bring oneself into another's good graces
**h.** feeling of sickness
**i.** great force
**j.** fake

**B.** *Synonyms* are words with similar meanings. Choose the synonym that is most similar in meaning to the Vocabulary Word in bold type. Write the letter of that synonym in the space provided.

_____ 11. **embark:** (a) leave  (b) harden  (c) board  (d) arrive

_____ 12. **undulating:** (a) flat  (b) wavy  (c) tempting  (d) soft

_____ 13. **sullen:** (a) gloomy  (b) happy  (c) confused  (d) ill

_____ 14. **furtively:** (a) secretively  (b) dishonestly  (c) calmly  (d) cleverly

_____ 15. **knoll:** (a) valley  (b) storm  (c) alarm bell  (d) hill

_____ 16. **dolefully:** (a) forgetfully  (b) joyfully  (c) sorrowfully  (d) pleadingly

_____ 17. **truculently:** (a) cruelly  (b) loudly  (c) noisily  (d) sadly

_____ 18. **insolence:** (a) creativity  (b) admiration  (c) deceit  (d) disrespect

_____ 19. **precipices:** (a) ditches  (b) mountains  (c) cliffs  (d) hurricanes

_____ 20. **subaltern:** (a) chief  (b) subordinate  (c) commander  (d) equal

Treasure Island

Name _____ Date _____

# TEST — PART I: OBJECTIVE QUESTIONS

**In the spaces provided, mark each true statement *T* and each false statement *F*. (16 points)**

_____ 1. Jim Hawkins finds a treasure map washed up on the beach.

_____ 2. Billy Bones suffers a stroke after Pew gives him the black spot.

_____ 3. Jim Hawkins learns of the pirates' plans for mutiny while hiding in a sea-chest.

_____ 4. Captain Smollett is shot and dies in a skirmish with the pirates at the stockade.

_____ 5. All by himself, Jim Hawkins boards the *Hispaniola*, kills a pirate, and recovers the ship.

_____ 6. Dr. Livesey surrenders the stockade to the pirates and gives them the treasure map.

_____ 7. Ben Gunn dug up the treasure long before the pirates landed on the island.

_____ 8. Long John Silver is taken aboard the *Hispaniola* and returned to England.

**Complete each statement by writing the letter of the best answer in the space provided. (14 points)**

9. As the novel begins, Jim Hawkins is living _____.
   a. in the home of Dr. Livesey
   b. at the Admiral Benbow Inn
   c. aboard the *Hispaniola*
   d. at the Spy-glass

10. Jim Hawkins and his mother go through Billy Bones's sea-chest looking for _____.
    a. the treasure map
    b. gold and jewels
    c. his will
    d. money

11. During the voyage to Treasure Island, the first mate, Mr. Arrow, _____.
    a. gets drunk and falls overboard
    b. sings about a mysterious pirate ship
    c. conspires with Long John Silver to mutiny
    d. takes over command of the ship

12. Ben Gunn is a former member of Captain Flint's crew who _____.
    a. joins Long John Silver and his pirate crew
    b. saves the life of Long John Silver
    c. takes Jim to his cave and shows him the treasure
    d. has been marooned on the island for three years

13. Jim Hawkins kills the pirate Israel Hands _____.
    a. on board the *Hispaniola*
    b. during the pirates' attack on the stockade
    c. during the fight at the site of the buried treasure
    d. accidentally, on the wharf

14. _____ is the favorite cry of Long John Silver's parrot.
    a. "Yo-ho-ho, and a bottle of rum!"
    b. "Dead men don't bite!"
    c. "Avast ye, matey!"
    d. "Pieces of eight!"

15. On the voyage back to England, _____.
    a. Silver escapes with some of the treasure
    b. the three mutineers escape
    c. Israel Hands is killed
    d. Jim begins to record the adventure

Study Guide | **53**

Name _____ Date _____

# TEST  PART II: SHORT-ANSWER QUESTIONS

**Answer each question, using the lines provided.** *(40 points)*

**16.** As they plan their voyage, why does Dr. Livesey advise Trelawney and Jim to keep quiet about their plans?

**17.** How does Jim Hawkins first learn about the mutiny?

**18.** Why do Captain Smollett, Dr. Livesey, and Squire Trelawney abandon the ship in favor of the stockade?

**19.** What does Jim do when he sneaks away from the stockade following the fight with the pirates?

**20.** After Jim finds the *Hispaniola* adrift and climbs on board, what does he discover has happened to the two pirates?

Name _____ Date _____

# TEST — PART II: SHORT-ANSWER QUESTIONS *(Continued)*

**Answer each question, using the lines provided.**

**21.** What happens to Jim when he returns to the stockade after capturing the *Hispaniola?*

**22.** After Jim's capture, why does Silver protect Jim from the other pirates?

**23.** Why does Dr. Livesey give the treasure map to the pirates?

**24.** How does Ben Gunn delay the pirates as they go to recover the treasure?

**25.** What happens to Silver during the voyage home?

Name _____ Date _____

# TEST — PART III: ESSAY QUESTIONS

**Choose *two* of the following topics. Use your own paper to write two or three paragraphs about each topic you choose.** *(30 points)*

1. "The Power of Greed" is an important **theme** in *Treasure Island*. Are all of the characters afflicted with greed? To what extent? Give examples to support your answer.

2. Jim Hawkins makes impulsive decisions, but somehow he manages to come out a winner. Long John Silver carefully plans his actions, but he ends up a loser. What do you think accounts for the difference in their success? Which manner of acting do you prefer? Explain.

3. Jim is characterized as feeling gloomy at the end of the novel. Why do you think his experiences have left him depressed rather than excited and pleased? Do you think his gloom will last? Give evidence from the novel to explain your answer.

4. In the **conflict** between two opposing forces in *Treasure Island*, the dutiful, or obedient, characters win and most of the violent ones end up dead or marooned. Why do you think Stevenson allows Long John Silver to escape the horrible end suffered by his mates?

5. Stevenson originally called this novel *The Sea Cook*. At the urging of his publisher, he changed it to *Treasure Island*. In your opinion, which is the better **title**? Use details from the story as you explain your answer.

**Use this space to make notes.**

# Answer Key

# Answer Key

*Treasure Island*

## Chapters 1–6: Making Meanings

> **READING CHECK**
> a. He seems to be avoiding certain people and to fear being found.
> b. Bones and Black Dog have a fight. Bones wins and chases Black Dog away, but Bones then suffers a stroke.
> c. The blind man grabs Jim with a painful grip, scaring Jim so that Jim takes him to see Bones.
> d. After they go to a neighboring hamlet for help and cannot get anyone to return to the inn with them, they go back home, get the key to Bones's sea-chest, open the chest, and search for money to cover Bones's debt to the inn.
> e. He gives the packet to Dr. Livesey. Jim thinks that the pirates were after the papers and that they must be important. He wants to put the papers into safe hands, and he trusts Dr. Livesey.

1. Most students may feel that he is unfriendly, crude, violent, and evil and they would not like to know him. Other students may suggest that they would like to get to know him because he would have fascinating stories to share.

2. Students should realize that the first-person point of view keeps the story "fresh," as viewed through Jim's eyes. That same point of view, however, limits the reader's knowledge to what Jim knows and understands. If the story were told from a limited third-person point of view, readers would not learn Jim's reactions and emotions firsthand, but they might see better what other characters are doing. If the story were told from the omniscient point of view, readers probably would understand more about the motivations of other characters.

3. Students may note that Dr. Livesey is serious, level-headed, competent, brave, and apparently honest.

4. The mood of civility, excitement, and security in the hall contrasts with the evil and insecure mood at the Admiral Benbow.

5. Most students will recognize the ideas that greed can be a motivating force and that the struggle between opposing forces can occur anywhere. Examples include Bones's attempt to keep the treasure for himself, and Pew's hurting and frightening Jim.

6. Answers will vary, but students may suggest that they might have seen through the pirates' deception more easily. Others may say that they would react as Jim does because they would also be ill at ease or scared.

7. Answers may include examples such as gambling, state lotteries, sweepstakes offered in the mail, and high-risk investments.

8. Students may suggest that a well-defined character helps to make the situation realistic and to provide a foundation for the actions and the characters that follow.

## Chapters 7–12: Making Meanings

> **READING CHECK**
> a. The squire bought a ship and hired a captain and crew.
> b. Silver looks like the man about whom Billy Bones, back at the Admiral Benbow Inn, had warned him. Furthermore, Jim sees Black Dog at Silver's tavern. Jim decides that Silver is not dangerous because Silver seems different from the buccaneers Jim has already met. Silver is friendly, companionable, and seemingly honest.
> c. Jim climbs into the barrel to get an apple. While inside, Jim overhears Silver explain his plans for mutiny to the other pirates.
> d. Silver points out that only the captain knows how to plot a course for the ship, that either Livesey or Trelawney has the map, and that the pirates don't know where the map is.

# Answer Key (continued)

*Treasure Island*

1. Most students will say that Silver is treacherous and unreliable. They also may recognize that he is a natural leader, able to motivate—and control—the sailors.

2. Circumstances are starting to change Jim slightly, but most students will suggest that he is still very much a boy.

3. Smollett is a dedicated man who is concerned for the safety of his crew and his ship. Like Dr. Livesey, he is practical and forceful.

4. Students may say that here Silver understands that he needs to keep the captain alive to plot a course and to navigate the ship. He also understands the crew and is both willing to kill for convenience and eager to keep control of the situation.

5. Many students may feel that Silver is acting friendly toward Jim to avoid suspicion, but some students may say that Silver genuinely likes Jim.

6. Students probably will be able to sympathize with Jim and to cite occasions when their hopes have been crushed. Their word choices to describe their feelings might include *depressed, disappointed, angry, furious, shocked, confused, cheated, mistreated,* and *sad.*

7. Answers will vary, but students may conclude that both friendship and animosity are proven ultimately by actions over time.

8. Students may recall that Smollett did not like the arrangement but was talked into accepting the crew. Since Trelawney does seem foolish, it is easy to see him taken in. Livesey is practical and shrewd, but he does not know sailors. It is also easy to believe that Silver is clever enough to deceive most people and that he could convince his followers to behave themselves.

## Chapters 13–21: Making Meanings

**READING CHECK**

a. Silver is trying to convince Tom to join the mutiny. When Tom refuses, Silver kills him.

b. Dr. Livesey decides that he and the others should give up the ship and take possession of the stockade. The stockade has water, which they lack on the ship.

c. The jolly-boat, overloaded with supplies and passengers, is swamped near the shore as Trelawney shoots at the pirates who are firing the cannon.

d. Silver wants the treasure map. He offers Smollett and the men a choice: He will guarantee their safe passage home, or they can remain on the island and he will send a ship for them.

e. Although they are outnumbered, Smollett's men are protected by the block-house, and they have plenty of guns and ammunition.

1. Student answers should include an awareness that the pirates lack discipline. They drink too much, quarrel among themselves, and lack the will to follow through with their plans.

2. Students who feel that Smollett was unwise will point to the deaths of the loyal seamen. Students who find the decision a wise one may say that Smollett and his men were outnumbered aboard ship, and that sending the crew ashore gave Smollett the time and opportunity to plan and make other moves.

3. Some students may find the narrators quite similar; others may feel that Jim is more intense and wide-eyed than the doctor.

4. Smollett maintains order—raising the flag, organizing the men, and filling out the log. Redruth is shot in the line of duty and dies.

5. The flag unites the men and stirs them to action against the pirates. The flag may symbolize England and home, order, justice, or goodness.

Study Guide | 59

# Answer Key (continued)

*Treasure Island*

6. Jim has become bolder and more willing to accept risks and to take matters into his own hands. He is less innocent and sees through the duplicity of others more easily.

7. Answers will vary, but ask students to explain how their questions would help them better understand the plot, characters, or themes of *Treasure Island*.

8. Students may suggest that mutiny often involves murder, that it causes injury and destruction, and that it is a betrayal of rightful authority.

9. Many students will say the shift is necessary so that the narrative can continue in the first-person point of view to describe the events that occur after Jim leaves the ship. Some students may have found the shift interrupting or confusing. Solutions might include allowing Jim to tell that part of the story in the third person, as one who has heard about the events later.

## Chapters 22–27: Making Meanings

**READING CHECK**
a. He leaves the stockade, armed and in possession of the treasure map.
b. Jim's coracle is swept against the side of the *Hispaniola*. After getting clear, Jim grabs a line dangling from the ship. He pulls himself up to the cabin window, looks inside, and sees two pirates fighting. His boat is swept by the current through the narrows and out to sea.
c. He climbs aboard and takes possession of the ship.
d. Jim agrees to bring Hands some rum, food, and a scarf to bind his wounds. Hands agrees to tell Jim how to sail the ship to shore. At this moment, they need each other.
e. When he sees a large fire, bigger than Captain Smollett would allow, he begins to wonder if something has gone wrong. Drawing closer, he hears people snoring. This sound is reassuring, which leads him to think that his friends must be there.

1. Some students may agree that it was a good decision because Jim was successful. Students who disagree may point out that Jim could have been killed and that he was lucky.

2. Many students will feel that Jim has been fortunate. For example, he awakens in the coracle to find the *Hispaniola* close by, and Hands's dirk fails to hit a vital part of his body.

3. Students probably will point to the struggle between Jim and Hands, and may conclude that it shows the self-destructive nature of violence.

4. Students should recognize that the surprise leaves the reader suspended, waiting to see what will happen next.

5. Students may point to any number of "fight scenes." Encourage them to be specific in their comparisons and conclusions.

6. Most students will agree that people give a lot of credit to "instinct," or "heart," or "gut feeling." They also may suggest that careful planning has its merits as well.

7. Answers will vary, but many students may suggest that villains are interesting because their commitment to wrongdoing seems out of the ordinary. Students also may suggest that Silver is interesting because he has some good qualities as well as evil ones.

## Chapters 28–34: Making Meanings

**READING CHECK**
a. The pirates give Silver the black spot. They blame him for not letting them kill the others and Jim now.
b. The pirates hear singing and think at first that it is Captain Flint. Then, they realize that it is Ben Gunn.
c. When the pirates find the empty hole and the treasure gone, they rebel against Silver. Livesey, Gray, and Gunn have hidden nearby, and they shoot two of the pirates. The others, except for Silver, run off.
d. It is in Gunn's cave. They load it onto the ship.

# Answer Key *(continued)*

## Treasure Island

1. Answers will vary. Students may complete sentences with the following answers.
   - . . . the pirates.
   - . . . be taken back to England and get off lightly with Dr. Livesey's help.
   - . . . the pirates turning on Long John Silver.

2. Silver's "game" is to survive by keeping "a foot in both camps"—that is, to keep open the option of returning to Captain Smollett by protecting Jim even while trying to keep the mutineers together and recover the treasure. Students may explain that it is "remarkable" because it is very daring, very clever, or both.

3. Examples include the following: Jim honors his duty to Silver by not running off when Livesey suggests that he escape. The pirates fulfill their duty to their code of honor by allowing Silver to respond to their charges against him. Silver tells Smollett that he has returned to his "dooty."

4. The reader depends upon Jim to provide the answers; if Jim is baffled, the reader is also. The resulting uncertainty increases the tension in the story.

5. Students may suggest that Silver is such a strong, interesting character that Stevenson wants him to survive. Throughout, Silver has shown himself to be a survivor, and his escape is consistent with that.

6. Some students may suggest that Jim has high principles—that is, he probably feels that his word is more important than mere convenience—and so may not have found the choice hard. Other students may say that it would be hard for Jim to turn away from his true friends.

7. Ben Gunn certainly is a "fool," for he squanders his share of the treasure in less than three weeks. No other characters are named in this matter, but Hawkins does say that those who shared in the treasure "used it wisely or foolishly, according to [their] nature."

8. Answers will vary. For example, some students may feel that the ending seems rushed. Other students, however, may think that Stevenson's ending is effective because it leaves open many possibilities for these characters.

## Exploring The Connections

### The Mildenhall Treasure
### Making Meanings

> **READING CHECK**
> a. It is pieces of table silver that a Roman family buried more than 1,500 years earlier.
> b. He finds it while plowing in a field.
> c. Ford convinces Butcher that it is just a lot of worthless old junk.
> d. The objects are claimed by the British Museum.

1. Answers will vary. Students may suggest that they would have turned it in immediately and claimed the reward.

2. Butcher is described as odd-looking, but peaceful and easy going. When he is cheated out of all but a very small reward, Butcher's lack of anger suggests both his lack of bitterness and his lack of malice.

3. Students may suggest that the Butchers wanted to avoid trouble or that they did not realize that they had any claim to the treasure.

4. In the early part of *Treasure Island,* young Jim Hawkins is very naive about people and is easily fooled by scoundrels. As he gathers experience, however, he develops better judgment. Hawkins is adventurous, curious, and quick thinking. Gordon Butcher is an adult, but he, too, seems naive about people. Unlike Hawkins, he avoids adventure, is not very inquisitive, and does not think quickly.

# Answer Key (continued)

## Treasure Island

5. Because Livesey is honest and reliable, he probably would have dealt fairly with Butcher. Livesey probably would have reported the find immediately and then seen to it that Butcher shared in the reward. Students should remember, too, that Butcher is content with his life and does not seem unhappy with the way that things turn out for him.

6. Many students will say that Ford was guilty of trying to hide the discovery. Some will say that Butcher was innocent and should have gotten the full amount of the award, or at least the entire amount paid. Others will say that Butcher had reason to suspect that the treasure had some value and should have reported it to the police on his own. They might agree that the partial reward was fair compensation.

7. Some students will consider the law unfair. The finder, especially if the person owns the land, should be able to keep possession. Other students may conclude that the law is fair. Since these items have historic value, they belong to the British people rather than to any one person.

8. Answers will vary. Some students may feel that Dahl should have tried harder to get other people's accounts. Without this input, there is no way of knowing whether the story is accurate. Other students will say that he wrote truthfully because he gave Ford an opportunity to tell his side of the story, but Ford refused to do so.

## "We Found It! We Found It!"
## Making Meanings

> **READING CHECK**
> a. Estimates ranged as high as $400 million.
> b. Fisher found a part of the wreckage that had been displaced by a hurricane. He explored that location for some time before realizing that it was not the main site.
> c. Fisher's son Dirk and Dirk's wife, along with another diver, died during a storm at sea.
> d. Fisher used salvage boats and skilled divers to search the ocean floor. High-tech equipment identified likely locations and searched for signs of shipwrecks. Research of documents in Spain helped establish possible sites of the wreck.

1. Many students will say that they would not be surprised. Some governments have laws guaranteeing them first right to the found treasure. Other students will feel that the state has no right to a claim upon treasure that is found through someone else's hard work.

2. Details will vary, but students may conclude that Wilentz depicts Fisher as determined, persistent, optimistic, cheerful, committed, and adventurous. He continues the search despite the loss of his son and daughter-in-law. He searches for seventeen years.

3. Students probably will feel that the treasure hunters' reasons were the same—namely, they all wanted to find wealth.

4. Students might point to the time that Fisher devoted to the search or his persistence despite disappointments to suggest themes that relate to hard work and perseverance.

5. Answers will be personal and need not be shared. Students might want to spend some time with their writer's notebook, exploring how they might make their dreams come true.

# Answer Key (continued)

*Treasure Island*

## *Tiger Moran's Loot:* Making Meanings

> **READING CHECK**
> a. They were members of Tiger Moran's criminal gang.
> b. They want Sam to help them find Tiger Moran's hidden treasure.

1. Many students might express reservations about searching for wealth that came from criminal activity. Other students might welcome the chance to join these treasure hunters; there is a good amount of treasure to share. Furthermore, Gramps seems a knowledgeable, reliable leader.

2. Gramps, a former gangster, still has connections with old mobsters, like Sudden Sam. He also is a responsible adult who looks after the safety of the young people with him.

3. Examples of informal speech include "Kids, this here is Sudden Sam" and "How come you wasn't on the television with that fellow if he come here to see you?" This informal speech helps make the scene true to life, for the characters talk as some people actually speak.

4. The groups are similar. The young people in Myers's story are counterparts for Jim Hawkins in the novel. They're young like Jim, but probably more worldly-wise. Gramps and Sudden Sam are old gangsters who are similar to the pirates of *Treasure Island*. Tiger Moran also seems to be a parallel to Stevenson's Captain Flint. Most students will say that the characters in this excerpt appear less threatening and dangerous than the pirates in *Treasure Island*.

5. Many students will comment that it is possible that gangsters hid treasure, perhaps intending to return for it but being captured first. Other students may suggest that the gangsters would be more likely to spend it, hide it in banks in Switzerland, or invest it.

## *Return to the* Titanic: Making Meanings

> **READING CHECK**
> a. They travel in the *Alvin,* a small submarine capable of diving to great depths.
> b. They use *JJ,* a small underwater robot.
> c. Items include chinaware, wine bottles, chamber pots, bathtubs, an unbroken chandelier, the head of a china doll, anchors, chains, bronze-topped capstans, and other parts of the ship.

1. Answers will vary. Students may respond that it made them feel sad, nostalgic, or thoughtful. Encourage them to provide reasons for their responses.

2. The explorers cannot take a chance on running out of battery power or oxygen, so they must follow the schedule rigidly. They are two miles deep in the ocean. They have no hope of rescue if they have trouble and cannot surface.

3. The *Alvin* might have fallen into the ship and been damaged or unable to get back out. Either possibility could have been disastrous for the crew.

4. Ballard's treasure is the *Titanic* itself and what he can see and learn about it. He is not seeking gold and silver or precious items, but knowledge. He takes nothing but pictures and memories back with him. Crew members of the *Hispaniola,* on the other hand, seek treasure.

5. Ballard doesn't reveal too much at once; rather, he lets us share his own uncertainty in a moment-by-moment recounting of his suspenseful search. The reader also wants to know exactly what he does find. His descriptions are powerful enough that we want to stay at his pace and not jump ahead.

Study Guide

# Answer Key (continued) — *Treasure Island*

6. Answers will vary. Students should express an understanding of the danger and discomfort of the adventure as well as the excitement of participating in such an adventure.

7. Some students will feel that it is a waste of money and dangerous as well. They might question whether any practical knowledge is gained from such expeditions. Other students might say that visiting such sites is valuable because it is a way to do historical research.

## Reading Skills and Strategies Worksheets

### Chapters 1–6: Describing Characters

Answers may vary. Sample answers are provided below.

| Character | Physical Description | Actions |
|---|---|---|
| Jim Hawkins | | waits on people at the inn; feels sorry at the deaths of his father and Bones |
| Jim's mother | | runs an inn; searches Billy Bones for money due the family, but no more |
| Billy Bones | "tall, strong, heavy, nut-brown"; pigtail; "soiled blue coat"; ragged and scarred hands; "black, broken nails"; scar on one cheek; "filthy, heavy, bleared scarecrow of a pirate"; wears a key | sings; drinks rum heavily; leaps at Black Dog; dies of a stroke |
| Black Dog | "pale, tallowy creature"; two fingers missing on left hand; wore a cutlass | talks heatedly with Billy Bones |
| Pew | blind man; carries stick to tap his way; wears "great green shade"; hunched; wears "huge old tattered sea-cloak with a hood, that made him appear positively deformed"; dreadful looking; "horrible, soft-spoken" | gives Billy Bones the black spot; instructs men who come to search Billy Bones's room; trampled by a horse |
| Dr. Livesey | "neat"; "bright, black eyes"; wears white-powdered wig | doctors Jim's father and Bones; smokes a pipe |
| Squire Trelawney | over six feet tall; broad; "bluff, rough-and-ready face, all roughened and reddened and lined"; black eyebrows which "moved readily" | interprets the account book; proposes they go after the treasure; pledges silence about the expedition |

### Chapters 7–12: Responding to Quotations

Answers may vary. Sample answers are provided below.

| Quotation | Response |
|---|---|
| "The squire has been talking, after all." | I knew he'd talk. What else will happen because the Squire talked? |
| ". . . let's see—Black Dog? No, I don't know the name, not I." | He's lying, I think. He's trying to pull more information out of Jim. |
| "I assure you I was quite of the squire's way of thinking, and hated the captain deeply." | Jim's wrong to hate the captain. The captain's right to be concerned about the crew. I'd want to quit if I were the captain, too. |
| "Pieces of eight!" | I wonder what that's all about? |
| "I want to go into that cabin, I do. I want their pickles and wines, and that." | Talk about greed; they just can't wait. They're a bunch of hotheads, too. |
| ". . . and out of these seven one was a boy, so that the grown men on our side were six to their nineteen." | Jim's wrong to think he won't be much help. Age doesn't really matter. He's proven his value already, anyway. |

*Treasure Island*

# Answer Key (continued)

*Treasure Island*

## Chapters 13–21: Tracking Plot Details

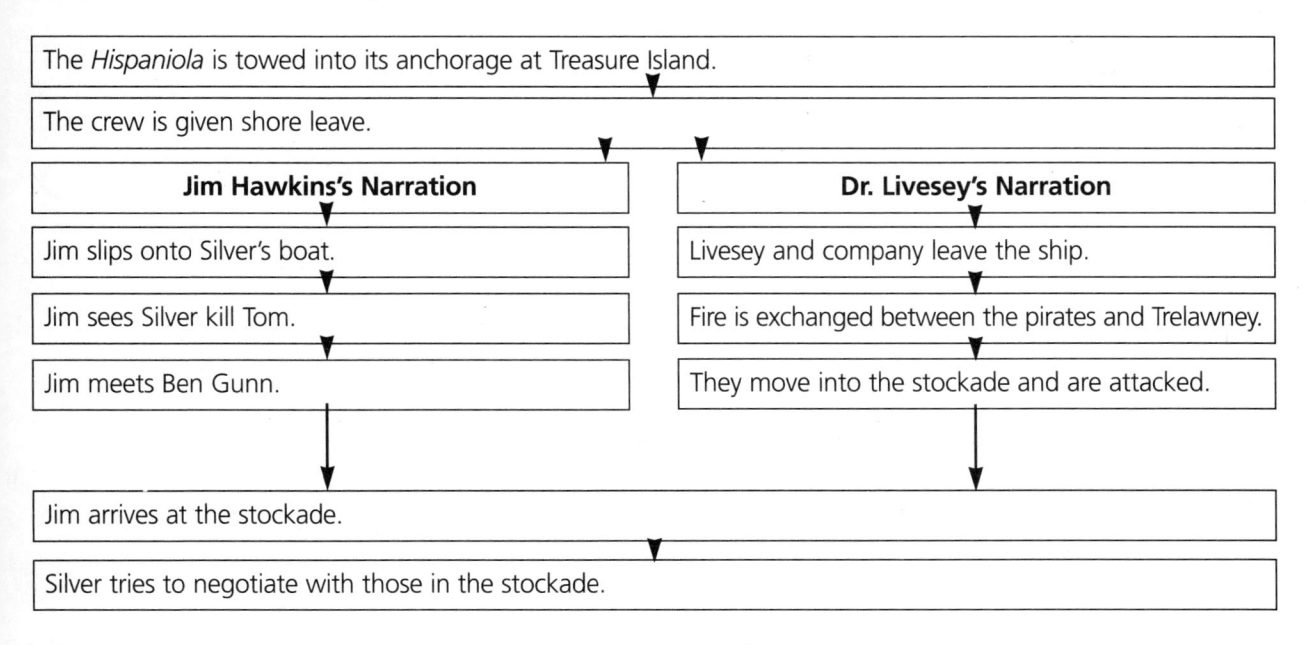

- The *Hispaniola* is towed into its anchorage at Treasure Island.
- The crew is given shore leave.

**Jim Hawkins's Narration**
- Jim slips onto Silver's boat.
- Jim sees Silver kill Tom.
- Jim meets Ben Gunn.

**Dr. Livesey's Narration**
- Livesey and company leave the ship.
- Fire is exchanged between the pirates and Trelawney.
- They move into the stockade and are attacked.

- Jim arrives at the stockade.
- Silver tries to negotiate with those in the stockade.

## Chapters 22–27: Identifying Problems and Solutions

Answers may vary slightly. Sample answers are provided below.

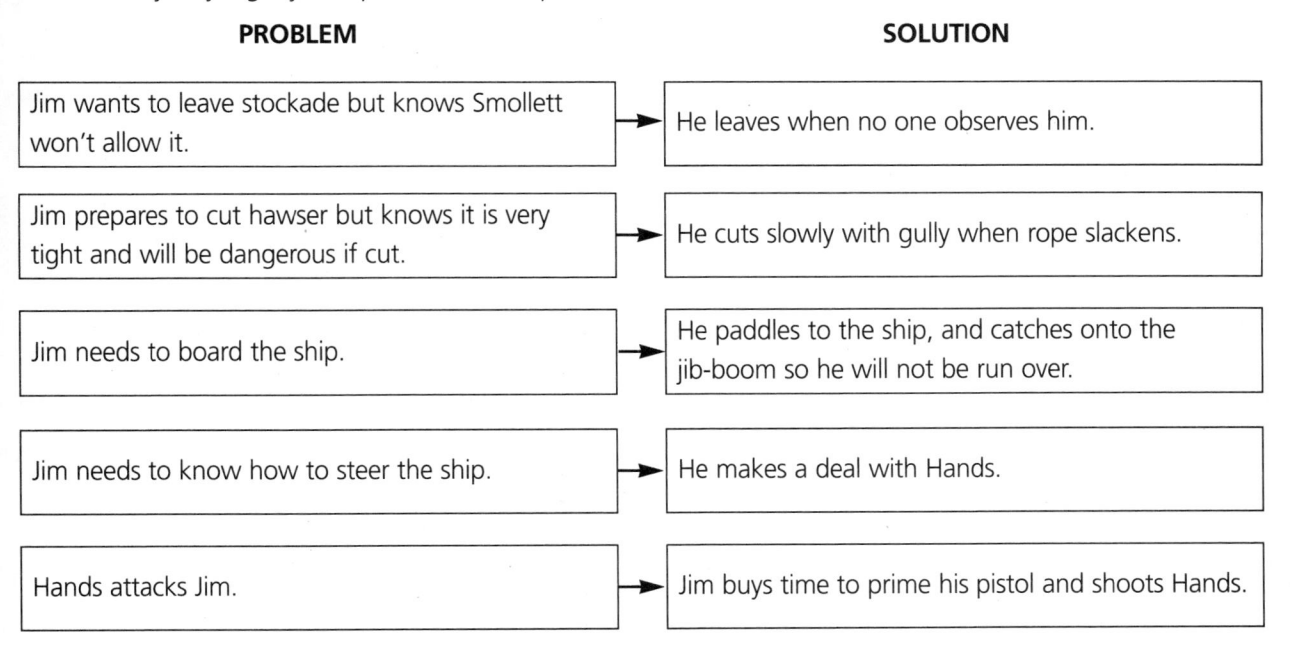

| PROBLEM | SOLUTION |
| --- | --- |
| Jim wants to leave stockade but knows Smollett won't allow it. | He leaves when no one observes him. |
| Jim prepares to cut hawser but knows it is very tight and will be dangerous if cut. | He cuts slowly with gully when rope slackens. |
| Jim needs to board the ship. | He paddles to the ship, and catches onto the jib-boom so he will not be run over. |
| Jim needs to know how to steer the ship. | He makes a deal with Hands. |
| Hands attacks Jim. | Jim buys time to prime his pistol and shoots Hands. |

Study Guide | 65

# Answer Key (continued) — *Treasure Island*

## Chapters 28–34: Analyzing Events

Answers may vary slightly. Sample answers are provided below.

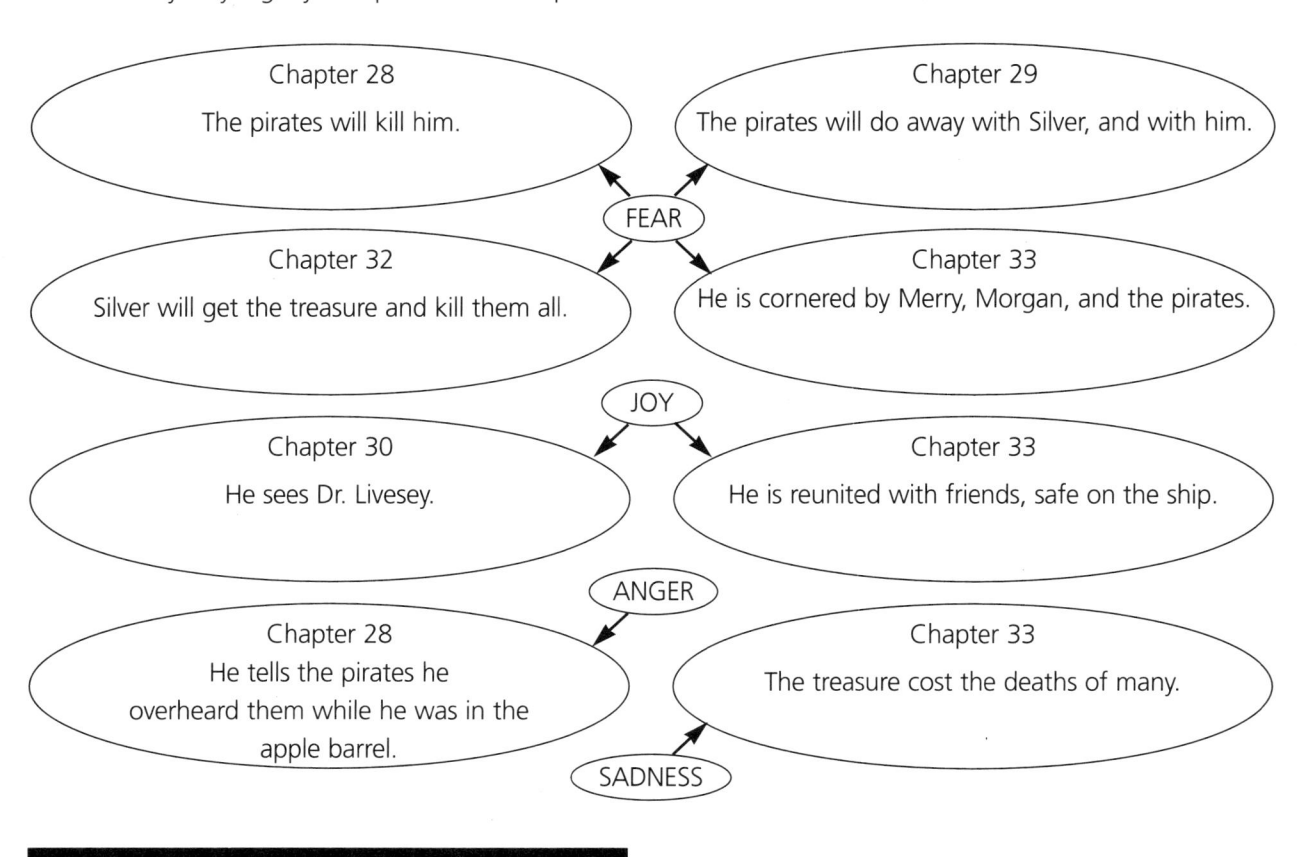

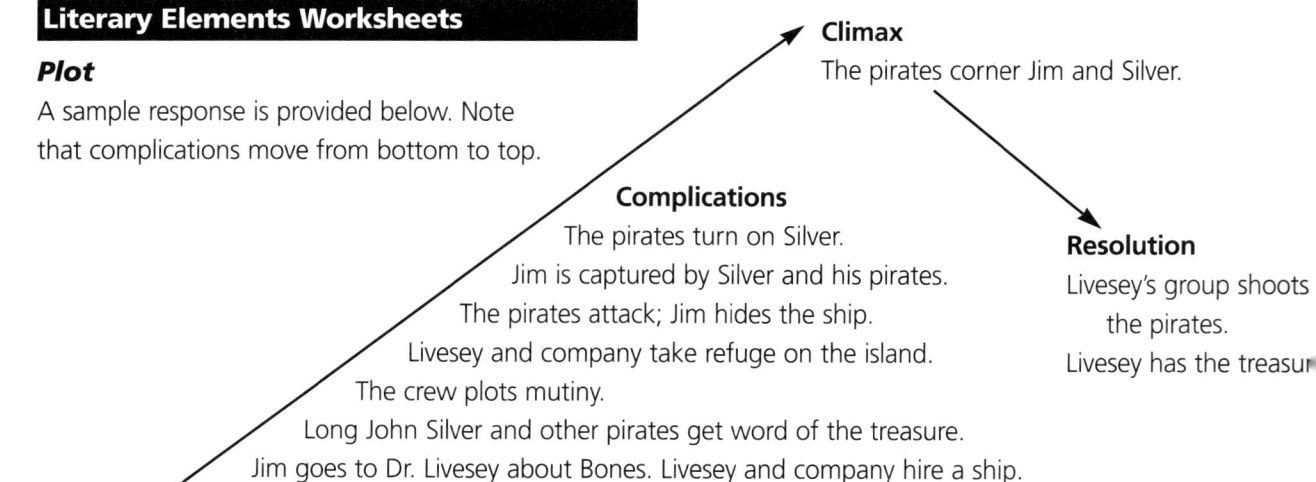

**Chapter 28** — The pirates will kill him. — FEAR
**Chapter 29** — The pirates will do away with Silver, and with him. — FEAR
**Chapter 32** — Silver will get the treasure and kill them all. — FEAR
**Chapter 33** — He is cornered by Merry, Morgan, and the pirates. — FEAR

**Chapter 30** — He sees Dr. Livesey. — JOY
**Chapter 33** — He is reunited with friends, safe on the ship. — JOY

**Chapter 28** — He tells the pirates he overheard them while he was in the apple barrel. — ANGER

**Chapter 33** — The treasure cost the deaths of many. — SADNESS

## Literary Elements Worksheets

### Plot

A sample response is provided below. Note that complications move from bottom to top.

**Climax**
The pirates corner Jim and Silver.

**Complications**
The pirates turn on Silver.
Jim is captured by Silver and his pirates.
The pirates attack; Jim hides the ship.
Livesey and company take refuge on the island.
The crew plots mutiny.
Long John Silver and other pirates get word of the treasure.
Jim goes to Dr. Livesey about Bones. Livesey and company hire a ship.
Pirates look to Bones for a treasure map. Bones dies.

**Resolution**
Livesey's group shoots the pirates.
Livesey has the treasure.

**Basic situation**
There is treasure on Treasure Island.

# Answer Key (continued)   *Treasure Island*

## Characterization

Answers may vary. A sample answer is provided below.

**What others say about him:**
Trelawney: He's a "man of substance"; he has a bank account he's never overdrawn

**What he says:**
"I'm bound I'll be good."
"I'm rich."

**Long John Silver's Characteristics**
intelligent
clever
looks out after his own interests
is willing to kill to get what he wants
has money and wants to get more

**What he does:**
is ship's cook
changes sides when it suits him
kills Alan and Tom

**What he looks like:**
left leg cut off at the hip
tall and strong
plain, pale face

## Conflict

Answers may vary. Sample answers are provided below.

| Character | Situation | Internal or External | Description of Conflict |
|---|---|---|---|
| Jim's mother | Going through Bones's money | external | She risks danger to get the money she feels is due her family. |
| Jim | Climbs aboard the drifting *Hispaniola* | external | He has to climb aboard or be swamped. |
| Silver | Handed the black spot | external | He has to figure out how to outfox the pirates. |
| Jim | Dr. Livesey offers to take Jim back to the other group. | internal | Jim wants to run but has promised Silver he will remain with the pirates. |
| Captain Smollett | Is in charge of a crew that plans mutiny | external | He has to plan how to outwit the crew. |
| Dr. Livesey | Leaves block-house | external | He could be killed by pirates trying to find Gunn. |
| Silver and Jim | The treasure has disappeared. | external | They confront the pirates who want to kill both of them. |

Study Guide | **67**

# Answer Key (continued)   *Treasure Island*

## Vocabulary Worksheets

### Vocabulary Worksheet 1: Chapters 1–12

If you wish to score this as a worksheet, assign the point values given in parentheses.

**A.** *(6 points each)*

1. abominable
2. derisively
3. obstinately
4. countenance
5. lee
6. buccaneer
7. prodigiously
8. indomitable
9. nautical
10. trades

**B.** *(5 points each)*

11. detestable
12. galley
13. quays
14. dexterity
15. lancet
16. rebuff
17. sinewy
18. rheumatics

### Vocabulary Worksheet 2: Chapters 13–34

If you wish to score this as a worksheet, assign the point values given in parentheses.

**A.** *(5 points each)*

1. i
2. j
3. g
4. f
5. d
6. e
7. c
8. h
9. b
10. a

**B.** *(5 points each)*

11. c
12. b
13. a
14. a
15. d
16. c
17. a
18. d
19. c
20. b

## Test

### Part I: Objective Questions

1. F
2. T
3. F
4. F
5. T
6. T
7. T
8. F
9. b
10. d
11. a
12. d
13. a
14. d
15. a

### Part II: Short-Answer Questions

16. Dr. Livesey fears that there will be people who will try to steal the map or beat them to the treasure.
17. He climbs into the apple barrel, where he overhears a conversation between Silver and members of the crew about the mutiny.
18. They can hold out longer against the pirates at the stockade because the stockade, unlike the ship, has a good supply of water.
19. He finds Gunn's boat, paddles out, and cuts the *Hispaniola* loose to drift.
20. The pirates have fought; one is dead and Hands is severely wounded.
21. He is captured by the pirates who have moved into the stockade.
22. Silver hopes that if he saves Jim's life, Jim will protect him from execution if Silver is later captured and returned to England.
23. He knows that the map is useless because Ben Gunn already has recovered the treasure.
24. He sings a song and makes them think it is the ghost of Captain Flint.
25. He jumps ship and disappears.

# Answer Key *(continued)*

## *Treasure Island*

### *Part III:* Essay Questions

Students should respond to two out of the five essay topics. Answers will vary, but all should include specific references to the text.

1. Students should be aware that greed is a motivating factor for most of the characters in the book, although they are affected by it to varying degrees. The pirates, for example, are obsessed with greed and willing to do anything to obtain the treasure. Jim, Dr. Livesey, and Squire Trelawney also are driven by greed, as shown by their speed in planning their voyage. Unlike the pirates, however, they are not blinded by greed; they retain a sense of humanity.

2. Jim is lucky. For example, he falls asleep in the apple barrel and wakes up to hear the talk of mutiny. He falls asleep in the coracle and wakes up to find himself almost on top of the *Hispaniola,* where one pirate is already dead and the other is seriously wounded. Jim's decisions may be rash, but he is lucky and so things turn out well. Silver loses in part because he has chosen greedy crew members and in part because he is unlucky. His crew cannot function because they are drunk. Two of his crew, who are supposed to be protecting the ship, attack each other. His conversation is overheard by a young boy asleep in an apple barrel. The treasure is obtained first by a confused sailor who was marooned on the island. Most students will prefer to be lucky, but most should recognize the need for good planning.

3. The question of Jim's mood is problematic. Students who have a good grasp of the novel as a "coming of age" story about Jim may point out that Jim's adventures have pushed him beyond the narrow view of childhood and into an adult view that includes recognition of the potential for evil in people. Such a discovery is bound to hit a rather innocent young person very hard, but Stevenson suggests that Jim's feelings will mellow as he grows older.

4. Students may suggest that Silver is not a completely evil character, but that he displays some good qualities. Silver is also the most intriguing character in the novel—crafty, determined, entertaining, and a survivor. Perhaps Stevenson did not want to kill off this interesting character. Other students may suggest that Silver must survive as a symbol of violence because the struggle against violence in the world is not at an end just because this particular story has concluded.

5. Some students will say *The Sea Cook* is the better title because it is the name of the novel's most interesting character. Others may say that *Treasure Island* is a better title because the novel is about treasure, the adventure of searching for treasure, and how that search affects each character.

# Notes